THE

FOURTH EDITION

ENTREPRENEUR'S
GUIDE TO EQUITY
COMPENSATION

David Binns

Martin Staubus

Ron Bernstein

The Beyster Institute at the Rady School of Management
University of California, San Diego

This publication is designed to provide accurate and authoritative information regarding the subject matter. It is sold with the understanding that the Beyster Institute does not provide legal, tax or accounting advice. The information contained here does not constitute legal advice on the design or implementation of equity compensation plans, nor is it intended as a guide to implementation. Equity compensation plan design and implementation is a complex undertaking, and legal, tax, and/or accounting advice should be sought before designing and implementing any type of equity compensation plan.

Written and published by the Beyster Institute at the Rady School of Management, UC San Diego, La Jolla, CA
Email: info@beysterinstitute.ucsd.edu
Web: http://beysterinstitute.ucsd.edu
ISBN: 0-9664077-7-6
Library of Congress No. 2006922320
Authors: David Binns, Martin Staubus, and Ron Bernstein

Editor: Debra Sherman

Table of Contents

Foreword

This 4th edition of *The Entrepreneur's Guide to Equity Compensation* is designed to make equity compensation more relevant and understandable for all business executives. The approaches and principles discussed inside are applicable no matter whether a company is large or small, in a start-up, high growth or mature stage, or wanting executive-oriented or broad-based incentives.

Tax law changes enacted prior to 2006 are reflected in this new edition as are the 2005 changes to stock option accounting rules. Other topics include ESOPs in S Corporations, international equity compensation plans and making ownership real for employees.

The Entrepreneur's Guide was written by the employee ownership consulting staff of the Beyster Institute at the Rady School of Management, University of California, San Diego. It is intended to be a useful guide for entrepreneurs, executives, advisors, investors, and anyone else wishing to learn about using equity compensation effectively. *The Entrepreneur's Guide* is based on practical experience gained from helping hundreds of entrepreneurs and executives sort through the issues involved in designing and implementing employee stock programs. This book is the result of lessons learned and best practices observed.

The Beyster Institute, a non-profit organization dedicated to fostering entrepreneurship, employee ownership and participation worldwide, stands at the forefront of the employee ownership movement. The Institute hosts educational forums, confers with colleagues across multiple disciplines related to compensation and motivation, consults with hundreds of companies considering and implementing equity-based compensation plans, and of course, develops publications like *The Entrepreneur's Guide.*

The Institute's vision is based on the leadership of our founder, Dr. J. Robert Beyster, who also founded and led Science Applications International Corporation (SAIC) for 35 years. With Dr. Beyster at the helm, SAIC became a multi-billion dollar, Fortune 500, employee-owned company. Dr. Beyster began sharing stock ownership with employees upon SAIC's inception in 1969 because he felt it was only fair that those who contribute to building the company should own it in a manner consistent with their contribution. By allowing participation, innovation, and shared responsibility, he also encouraged entrepreneurial behavior in SAIC's 40,000+ employees. Convinced that the practice of sharing the wealth with employees who were strongly engaged in the business was the principal engine of SAIC's growth and success, Dr. Beyster started the Foundation for Enterprise Development in 1986 to help other companies use employee ownership effectively. In 2002, the Foundation for Enterprise Development launched the Beyster Institute.

Today, the Beyster Institute focuses on helping companies succeed by combining the values of entrepreneurship with employee ownership. Countless examples of successful companies, numerous detailed research studies, and our own consulting experience over a 20-year period bear out the effectiveness of this approach.

Introduction

It's a little like this: you've entered a boat race, but you aren't given a boat. Instead, you're given a load of boat-building materials which, before your eyes, are tossed into the water. To start the race, you have to jump in after them and build your own boat while treading water and dodging the sharks. First one to the far side of the bay wins.

That's entrepreneurship. It is a process of creating something where there was nothing. It demands the ability to work simultaneously *in* the business and *on* the business—that is, taking care of the daily operations while also attending to the growth and development of the larger enterprise. It is not for the faint of heart.

It is a competitive endeavor, and if you can't out-perform the others, you get nowhere. And what's especially challenging—maddening, frustrating and downright devilish at times—is that the outcome is so very much not just in your own hands. Unless you plan to be a solo practitioner of some kind, building a business means operating through and with other people. The success of your venture will be determined not by your efforts alone but by the performance of the cast of people—employees, partners or associates—that you assemble.

So, if there is a strategy that can help you get more out of the people on whom you depend and also boost your organizational horsepower, you owe it to yourself to take a serious look. An employee ownership program that is designed and used wisely can be just that strategy.

By "employee ownership," we mean the practice of putting company equity into the hands of the people on whom the company counts to do the work. As you'll see in the pages ahead, there are a variety of different vehicles or methods for doing this, such as stock options, ESOPs (employee stock ownership plans), stock purchase arrangements, deferred compensation plans, "synthetic" equity and more.

The full spectrum of employee ownership vehicles is being used at an impressive number of companies today. ESOPs, for example, are now in operation at roughly 12,000 companies. As a group, these companies, most of them small-to-midsized privately held firms, have made stockholders of more than 10 million employees. Several thousand more firms have chosen other methods to put company stock in the hands of their employees. All told, nearly 40% of the employees of America's corporations now own stock in the company where they are employed.

And it's no mystery why so many companies have taken this route. There is ample evidence of the power of equity sharing to boost business performance.

Take the airline business, where Southwest Airlines is, as of this writing, worth more on the public market than all of America's big "legacy" airlines combined. It also happens that, unique among the major airlines, Southwest has granted stock options to its pilots, and every Southwest employee has a significant equity interest in the company.

At Starbuck's Coffee, which not only leads an industry but virtually invented it, those baristas are stock option holders, and personally benefit from company growth. Microsoft, decades younger than IBM, has left that business icon of a previous generation in its silicon dust, having built a global business powerhouse by putting as much as a third of the company's equity in the hands of the people it depends on to do the work. Indeed, the entire Silicon Valley phenomenon and the explosion of information technology was fueled by the drive, the creativity and the legendary long work hours of tech workers who, through employee ownership programs, were cut in on a share of the fantastic wealth they produced.

Academic research has borne out what these observations suggest. A study of 105 publicly traded companies that widely distribute stock options among their employees found that in the three years following the implementation of their option plans, the companies, on average, improved productivity by 17% and return on assets by 2.3% per year. An earlier study matching employee ownership companies with industry rivals that were comparable except for the employee stock program found that the equity sharing companies, on average, had boosted growth rates by 2% to 3%.

But improved performance is not as simple as just putting in an employee stock plan and reaping the benefits. Indeed, for every example of the kind cited above, there is an example of another company, such as United Airlines, that rolled out an equity compensation program and got nowhere.

Recall the study that found that the companies with employee stock programs had improved their growth rates by 2% to 3% over the control companies. When the researchers combed their data more closely, they discovered a fascinating refinement. Rather than forming a classic bell-shaped curve, the data on the companies with employee stock plans were actually clustered into two distinct groups. One group showed virtually no performance advantage at all over their conventionally owned peers; the other revealed a group of companies that were out-growing their peers by as much as 10% *per year.*

Realizing the gains that employee ownership can provide takes a combination of factors, including selecting the right plan, engaging employees in the business, and attending to the details, all of which will be discussed in the pages ahead. Reading this book will provide a valuable orientation that will help you to navigate through the sometimes complex world of employee ownership.

Chapter One presents an overview of the model that we have used successfully over time in our work with business leaders. We call it `The Journey of Equity Sharing.' This chapter enumerates the various ways to share equity with employees and the different motivations for doing so. It also points out that there is much more to equity sharing than simply putting a plan in place. It lays out a framework for the equity sharing process from start to finish.

Chapters Two, Three and Four comprise the section on "individual-based" plans. These types of plans permit the employer to target equity on a selective basis to individuals of the company's choosing, and in amounts that the employer wishes. Chapter Two deals with stock grants, which simply involve awarding shares of stock to employees. Chapter Three discusses stock purchase arrangements, which require employees to invest their own money in order to acquire shares of their employer's stock. Chapter Four addresses stock options, the classic equity compensation tool for the high-growth environment.

Chapters Five and Six deal with "company-wide" plans that are designed to be offered broadly to most or all of a company's employees. While the individual-based vehicles discussed in the preceding chapters may be used to grant equity to all employees, the legal terms governing company-wide plans require that the great majority of the sponsoring company's employees be included in the program. Two vehicles comprise this category: the "tax-qualified" employee stock purchase plan (ESPP), discussed in Chapter Five, and the employee stock ownership plan (ESOP), discussed in Chapter Six.

Chapters Seven and Eight explain how company-sponsored employee savings plans can be used to create an opportunity for employees to acquire stock in their employer. Chapter Seven is devoted to the use of 401(k) plans and other "defined contribution" retirement programs. Chapter Eight addresses the related area of "non-qualified" deferred compensation, an executive-level program that defers taxes and builds wealth for key employees.

Chapter Nine shows how a company that is unable or unwilling to transfer real company stock to employees can effectively simulate the financial benefits of employee stock ownership through "synthetic equity." Synthetic equity instruments such as stock appreciation rights and phantom stock deliver the economic benefits of stock ownership without employees actually owning the stock.

In Chapter Ten, we consider the challenges of extending equity compensation to employees at overseas operations. Multi-national equity plans require design and implementation strategies that differ from those for strictly domestic companies.

In the final section of the book, a range of key considerations is discussed. Chapter Eleven, Critical Issues, catalogs many of the important decisions that will have to be made in developing a plan. Chapter Twelve focuses on the process of culture-building and employee involvement that is necessary for plan success.

We recommend that along with looking at the various plan types, all readers review Chapter One, The Equity Sharing Journey; Chapter Eleven, Critical Issues; and Chapter Twelve, Getting the Most from Employee Ownership. These chapters are relevant no matter what type of plan is being considered.

Appendix A offers a discussion of how the choice of an equity compensation plan type may be affected by the legal form under which a business operates. Appendix B is a checklist to help with the development and implementation of an employee ownership plan.

A word about terminology. The practice by which companies make shares of their stock available to employees goes by a variety of names: equity sharing, employee stock ownership, equity compensation, stock compensation, equity ownership and others. While the definition of each term has slight nuances that may distinguish it from the others, in this book these terms will be used interchangeably. Also, throughout the book, the masculine pronoun is used to refer to employees or business owners in general. This is being done for the sake of simplicity and it should be understood to mean men and women alike.

While reading, take time to jot down thoughts and questions. They will serve as a map for continued exploration of employee ownership. The Beyster Institute can help answer questions, as can other professionals in the field. Our offices are located in San Diego, CA and in Washington, DC. Take a look at our web site, located at http://beysterinstitute.ucsd.edu, and feel free to contact us by phone or email.

Beyster Institute	Washington, DC office
San Diego office	UC Washington Center
1241 Cave St.	1608 Rhode Island Ave. NW
La Jolla, CA 92037	Washington, DC 20036
858/822-6000	202/833-4617
mstaubus@beysterinstitute.ucsd.edu	dbinns@ beysterinstitute.ucsd.edu

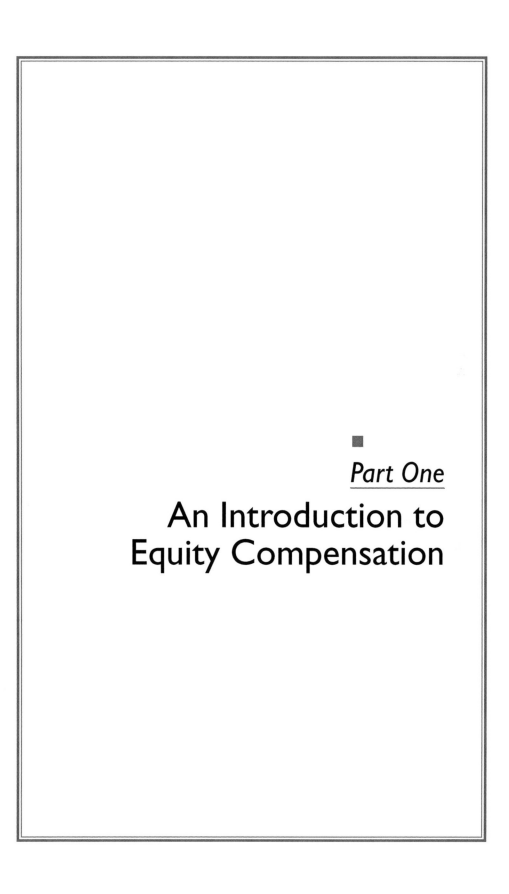

Part One

An Introduction to Equity Compensation

Chapter One

The Equity Sharing Journey

When implemented wisely, equity compensation can lead to a win-win-win situation: the company becomes more productive and competitive, shareholders gain liquidity and employees gain an ownership stake in their company, with the opportunity to use their talents and energy to create wealth for themselves.

The basic assumption in this scenario is that employees who own an interest in their company will be more motivated and more committed to producing successful outcomes for the company, and that this will help the company outperform its more conventional competitors. Reduced to specifics, the idea underlying employee ownership is that ownership will lead to changes in the attitudes of employee-shareholders and these attitude changes will in turn lead to better, more productive behaviors. It's what we at the Beyster Institute call "thinking and acting like an owner."

But creating an organization in which the people demonstrate ownership attitudes and behaviors is no simple task. It is an endeavor that requires dedication, effort and perseverance on the part of company leadership.

Implementing an employee ownership program is much less like throwing a switch than it is like setting out on a hiking expedition across the mountains. It can be somewhat daunting but with a clear destination, a good map, and markers that help point the way, it can be done. Indeed, it's been done many times, and the track record of the companies that have done it is flat out impressive. The very substantial rewards of this journey make it well worth the effort.

At the Beyster Institute, we have helped hundreds of companies navigate this journey. Based on our experience, we have developed a seven-step approach that provides guidance and direction for owners and executives who are interested in sharing stock ownership with employees. The seven steps ask you to:

1. Define a vision and objectives for equity sharing
2. Address owners' fears and concerns about equity sharing
3. Review the available tools for sharing equity
4. Select the right tools and create the program
5. Implement the program
6. Teach employees to think and act like owners
7. Attend to regular maintenance

STEP 1: DEFINE A VISION AND OBJECTIVES FOR EQUITY SHARING

The most critical step in developing an equity compensation plan is to define the business goals and objectives for the company and determine how the adoption of an equity compensation plan will support those objectives. The owner needs to answer the critical question: "What am I trying to achieve in my company by using equity compensation?"

While not all-inclusive, the answers might be reflected in the following list:

- Recruit and retain top employees.
- Reward high performance.
- Motivate employees to achieve business goals.
- Provide compensation on tax-advantaged terms.
- Allow everyone to benefit when the company does well.
- Share the wealth fairly with those who help generate it.
- Encourage all employees to think and act like owners.
- Raise capital.
- Provide liquidity to an owner on tax-advantaged terms.
- Finance an employee buyout.
- Facilitate a corporate divestiture.

It is important to be as specific as possible when identifying the objectives that an equity compensation plan should achieve. Prioritizing these objectives will help determine which equity compensation strategies are most appropriate for the company.

Along with determining goals and objectives, it is important to think about employee ownership relative to the company's vision. In other words, how does employee ownership fit into the overall business plans?

Strategic Plans and Liquidity Goals

The company's plans with regard to its own duration will factor heavily into decisions about its employee ownership approach. Is it a technology start-up that plans to be around only long enough to prove the worth of a new technology before being acquired or going public? Or is it a "built to last" company that sees a long future for itself going well into the next generation and beyond? Being in it for the long haul may require a different set of choices than hoping to go public or sell the company in a relatively short period of time.

Corporate Culture and the Employment Relationship

One of the significant benefits of employee ownership is that it can galvanize the workforce to focus on company performance. When equity is used as a reward for achievement, a program can also enhance individual performance. It is difficult, however, to achieve high levels of corporate performance without a) a team-oriented approach in which employees coordinate and cooperate toward the attainment of company goals, and b) an informed workforce that understands the goals and strategy of the company and how their own jobs affect the bottom line. One of the factors that should influence the employee ownership decision, then, is management's ability and willingness to create a culture that fosters knowledge and involvement. The stronger the commitment is to this kind of organization, the greater the likelihood of a successful employee ownership program.

STEP 2: ADDRESS OWNERS' FEARS AND CONCERNS ABOUT EQUITY SHARING

Owners of privately held companies are often concerned that having employees as shareholders could lead to the disclosure of confidential information about company business. There may be concern about the disclosure of financial information of a personal nature, such as the owner's compensation, or that as shareholders, employees could gain access to information that competitors could use to the detriment of the company.

In general, the right of a company shareholder to receive information about the company is governed by state corporate law. While the exact terms of a shareholder's rights may vary somewhat from state to state, it can safely be said that such rights do not typically go beyond the receipt of annual financial statements and, upon request, the identity of fellow shareholders. With few requirements regarding access to information, the company usually decides how much or how little to provide. However, the companies that experience the greatest performance boost from employee ownership are those that empower their employees to make better decisions by keeping them informed on the relevant factors.

Another fear that may be raised by owners as they consider the idea of employee stock ownership is that their ability to control the affairs of the company could be compromised in some fashion. Some owners are prepared to implement employee ownership only if they can maintain more than 50% ownership of the company, thereby assuring voting control. Others have concerns that the "minority shareholder rights" that are available in most states could lead to problems. Many have largely dismissed these concerns, concluding that control has more to do with leadership than legal rights. After all, it is hard to imagine that there is much of a future for a company in which the leader must resort to formal legal powers to govern the organization. The differences between these viewpoints are largely philosophical and are best addressed by talking to other company owners who have dealt with this issue. Voting rights are further discussed in Chapter Eleven.

The most significant emerging trend in the employee ownership arena today may well be the practice of "open book management." This method of managing a business focuses on training employees to understand the operation's financial workings so they can manage their own work with an eye toward their impact on the bottom line. In essence, the focus of leaders at the highest performing employee ownership companies is not on how to *minimize* employee access to business information but how to *maximize* it. Rather than hiding financial information, management is now insisting that employees learn it.

STEP 3: REVIEW THE AVAILABLE TOOLS FOR SHARING EQUITY

A diverse selection of equity sharing vehicles is available to any business that wants to give its employees an equity stake in the company. Indeed, new vehicles—or twists on old ones—seem to emerge with each change in the economy or the tax code. Identifying the vehicle—or set of vehicles—that is best suited to a company's unique goals and circumstances is critical to the design of a successful equity compensation plan.

The available vehicles may be divided into two groups. The first includes those that allow the company discretion in deciding who will receive equity awards and in what amount. They can also be used to distribute equity broadly throughout the organization. This group of equity-sharing vehicles, known as individual-based plans, includes:

- Stock options.
- Stock grants.
- Direct stock purchases.
- Stock appreciation rights and phantom stock.

The advantage of these plans is that they are very flexible and relatively inexpensive to implement. They are especially effective as incentives tailored to certain individuals or teams and may be linked to specific performance targets.

The other group of equity-sharing vehicles, termed broad-based plans, consists of equity plans that have been expressly designed to cover all or most of a company's workforce. The distinction of the broad-based plans is that the laws governing them make the broad distribution of the equity a legal requirement. There are strict rules regarding how these plans may be structured, and they may not be tailored to specific individuals or teams based on performance. This group includes the following vehicles:

- Tax-qualified Employee Stock Purchase Plan (ESPP).
- 401(k) plan.
- Employee Stock Ownership Plan (ESOP).

While these plans are less flexible than the individual-based ones, they can foster team-oriented attitudes, and offer significant tax advantages that the individual-based plans do not.

STEP 4: SELECT THE RIGHT TOOLS AND CREATE THE PROGRAM

Three factors influence equity compensation plan design: ownership vision, strategic business objectives, and practical considerations.

Ownership Vision

A well-designed employee ownership plan will be carefully aligned with company leadership's vision for the future of the venture. For a start-up technology company, for example, the equity program may be designed to address the firm's need to attract and retain talented employees who will work full-tilt toward a "liquidity event" (sale of the company or IPO) within a few short years. For others, the vision may be more philosophical: to build an employee-owned company, where employees are motivated to contribute to the long-term growth and success of the company and where those who make meaningful contributions are rewarded with a proportionate share of the equity.

Strategic Business Objectives

Plan design is also affected by the company's strategic business objectives. Financial strategy, for example, may dictate that a company priority is to minimize the consumption of cash. By offering equity as a form of compensation, it may be possible to reduce cash compensation below what would otherwise be required to recruit and retain qualified people. Likewise, human resources strategy may place the focus of recruiting efforts on those with an entrepreneurial spirit and enough confidence in their abilities to accept a stake in the company's growth in lieu of high cash compensation.

PRACTICAL CONSIDERATIONS

While big-picture factors like leadership vision and strategic objectives should be primary drivers of equity plan design, a diverse range of practical considerations will typically bear on the process as well. Such considerations may include industry trends, workforce profile, tax and accounting concerns, and the desire of current owners for liquidity. Here are a few of the common ones:

- **Ownership:** Who owns the company and what are their attitudes about sharing ownership? Is voting control an issue? Since current owners must approve an equity-sharing plan, it is important to have a clear picture of how equity compensation will be used to help the company meet future growth targets.

- **Capital:** What is the capital structure of the company? Does the company need capital? Will the company be seeking outside investors in the near future? How will future investors view the equity compensation program?

- **Growth:** What is the growth projection of the company? Owning stock in a start-up with great potential or a young company in a fast-growth mode may be a riskier proposition for employees than in a more established company with slower but steady growth.

- **Culture:** What is the company culture? Equity programs should be designed to reinforce the desired company culture. For example, individually focused equity incentives could be counterproductive in a company that is largely team based.

- **Workforce:** What is the profile of the company's workforce? Age and education are factors that must be considered in developing the plan. For a young workforce, more immediate stock awards may provide greater motivation, whereas for an older workforce, providing equity through retirement vehicles may be more appropriate. Employees' level of education and availability of cash become factors for any company that plans to offer shares to employees for purchase.

- **Industry:** What is the nature of the industry? What types of compensation programs are competitors using? In some industries, employees expect equity compensation as an industry standard; in others, employees may be skeptical.

Based on the factors discussed above, a "short list" of equity-sharing vehicles should emerge as those that are best suited to a company's particular needs.

The next step in mapping out an equity compensation plan is to take into consideration the potential positive and negative impact of the program on the company and employees. Factors to consider are:

- **Cost:** Will the program be cost effective for the company to implement and administer? Are there costs to employees and, if so, are they prohibitive enough to restrict participation?
- **Tax:** What are the tax implications—both positive and negative—for the company and the participating employees? Some equity awards can produce a large tax bill for the receiving employees without providing cash with which to pay those bills. This is particularly relevant when there is no ready market for employees to cash in shares to cover the potential tax liability.
- **Accounting:** How will the proposed methods affect the company's financial statements?
- **Motivation:** How will employees perceive the program? Is it designed to reinforce the company culture and reward behaviors critical to the company's future success? Will most employees perceive it as fair?
- **Management Support:** What are the attitudes of current owners, directors and managers toward employee ownership and its effect on corporate operations?

Other critical issues, detailed in Chapter Eleven, relate to securities registration, financial disclosure, stock pricing, stock restrictions and liquidity.

Lastly, before finalizing a proposed equity plan, get feedback on the plan from a variety of sources. This simply means talking about it: to employees, to colleagues, to other entrepreneurs who have shared equity, to the company's board of directors and to professionals in the field. This is also a time for insight and introspection to determine whether the plan will meet the owners' desired goals and objectives. In the complex process of creating a plan, it is particularly important at this stage to make sure the primary objectives are still being accomplished.

STEP 5: IMPLEMENT THE PROGRAM

Program implementation is a narrow but critical step in the process, best accomplished by retaining experienced professional advisors who can help with key decisions and draw up the necessary documents. If your regular company attorney is well-versed and experienced in employee stock ownership, by all means take advantage of that existing relationship. If this field is not a particular strong point for your regular attorney, do not hesitate to locate and retain a different attorney with a strong background in equity compensation. In addition to legal help, it may also be appropriate to talk to accountants, investment bankers, stock plan administrators and/or valuation firms.

STEP 6: TEACH EMPLOYEES TO THINK AND ACT LIKE OWNERS

All that has been recommended above is important, but it is not enough if the goal is to raise a company's level of business performance and become a more competitive organization. Studies of employee ownership as practiced at thousands of companies have made it clear that tapping into the promise of employee ownership takes more than simply passing out equity to employees.

Companies that have seen their performance jump as a result of turning employees into shareholders have consistently attended to the following responsibilities:

- **Educating employees to understand the company's system of employee ownership—what it is and how it works.** Employees won't be motivated by a mysterious, confusing program that was launched with a brief announcement and a memo written in legalese by an attorney.

- **Building a culture in which employee-owners are treated like the real shareholders they are.** Most humans are guided by their gut feelings and would feel that an owner is treated with decency and respect; therefore, if they are not treated that way they must not really be owners.

- **Giving employees information about how the company works and the numbers by which it is measured.** It's not enough to simply *want* the company to do well. For employee-owners to make a significant difference in the company's level of performance, they need the tools to make a real difference. Only with knowledge and information can people make the best decisions.

- **Encouraging employees to participate in the workplace.** Once employees are real owners, have knowledge about the company's business and its financial yardsticks, and are deeply motivated to see the company thrive, it can be a mistake to return to business as usual. The equity-sharing companies that have seen their bottom line performance jump have taken advantage of their better trained and more highly motivated workforce to make productive changes in the way the work gets done.

Commonly referred to as an ownership culture, this is the environment created by the companies that have truly succeeded at employee ownership. These companies enjoy a more stable workforce, greater profitability and enhanced value because of their ability to make ownership real to their employees.

STEP 7: ATTEND TO REGULAR MAINTENANCE

As we said earlier in this chapter, pursuing the strategy of employee ownership is a journey. Once the program has been launched, responsibilities still lie ahead. The big decisions will have been made, but certain areas should be attended to throughout the life of the plan: employee education, plan administration, and monitoring and reevaluation.

Plan administration will become an important responsibility once the plan is implemented. The company must choose to either keep administration in-house, which requires computerization and personnel, or to outsource it. Either way, good record keeping is essential.

The plan should be monitored and reassessed on a regular basis. Changes in the company, the industry or the regulatory environment may affect the plan's operation or its results. In addition, once the plan is implemented, revisions may still be needed.

Maintaining an effective equity compensation plan requires constant evaluation of the program. On a periodic basis, management should revisit the original objectives of the plan and solicit employee feedback to determine if it is still accomplishing the desired results. Over time, the rationale for the program may change based on internal dynamics, the marketplace or other factors. It may be necessary to adjust the program to accommodate changing circumstances and/or the objectives of the company and its workforce.

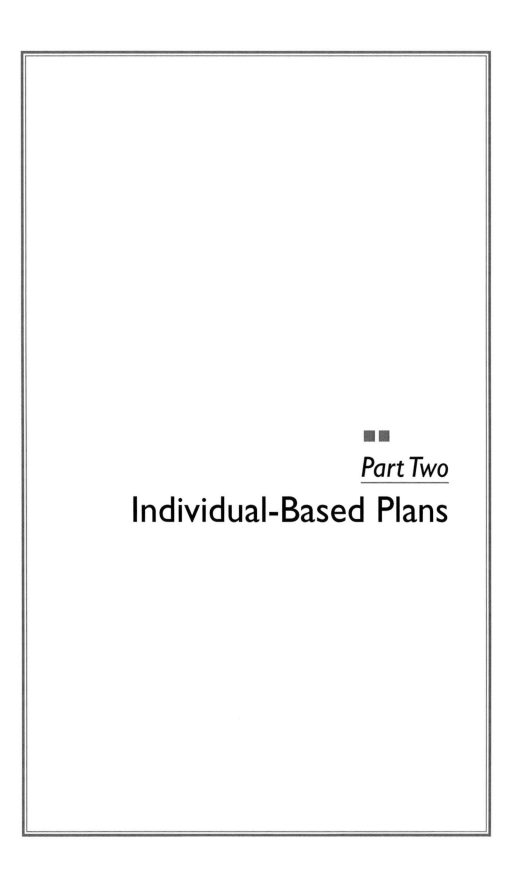

Part Two

Individual-Based Plans

Chapter Two

Stock Grants

Stock grants are one of the simplest and most flexible ways to award equity to employees. The low setup costs and ease of implementation make this equity vehicle attractive to companies of all sizes. However, because stock grants may have a significant tax impact on the receiving employees, they may not be well-suited to serve as the primary means for creating broad employee ownership. Grants of stock are, however, very effective as a supplement to other forms of equity sharing. They serve especially well as a reward for high performance or as part of an offer to attract key personnel.

HOW THEY WORK

Stock grants can take any of three common forms: vested grants, time-restricted grants and performance-restricted grants.

Vested Stock Grants. A vested stock grant is, very simply, an outright gift of stock from a corporation to an employee. Most commonly, such grants are made to key employees for achieving pre-established goals tied to company performance. For tax and accounting purposes, this award is treated essentially as a cash bonus (based on the fair market value of the stock) except that the award is in stock rather than cash.

Time-restricted Stock Grant. These are similar to vested stock grants but the award is restricted by a "vesting" provision which requires the employee to forfeit all or part of the award if his employment with the company ends prior to completing a specified period of service following receipt of the award. If the employee does in fact remain with the company for the required length of time, he gains full, unrestricted ownership of the shares. During the vesting period, the employee is considered to be the legal owner of the stock for purposes of any voting or dividend rights associated with the shares.

The vesting schedule that may be imposed on a restricted stock grant can provide that the shares will vest:

- All at once at the end of the vesting period, called "cliff vesting" or
- In incremental installments over the vesting period, called "graded vesting."

In either case, vesting provisions typically provide that a stock grant will be declared fully vested if the recipient should die or become permanently disabled, even if the grant would not otherwise have fully vested at that point. Many vesting provisions also provide that a stock grant will be declared fully vested upon a "change of control" (such as a sale of the company).

Performance-restricted Stock Grants. As with time-restricted grants, a performance-restricted stock grant takes the form of an award of shares that are provisionally transferred to an employee, but remain subject to possible forfeiture. In the case of performance-restricted grants, however, the risk of forfeiture does not lapse as a result of the passage of a certain amount of time, but only as a result of the individual or the company achieving some specified performance target. A typical performance target for an executive employee might tie a stock award to a certain amount of growth in the fair market value of the company—for example, when the company has increased in value by 50%, the award will be deemed fully vested (and the employee thus becomes free to sell the shares and pocket the cash proceeds).

USES OF STOCK GRANTS

Stock grants may be used in all the ways that cash bonuses are traditionally used in American businesses: for example, to reward employees for bringing in new business, managing a project under budget or meeting project goals. A start-up company might provide stock grants as part of an employee's annual compensation. This last use highlights the two special features that can make stock grants different and better than cash bonuses:

- **Stock grants help the company's cash position.** Not only does the use of stock as a bonus save the company the cash that it would otherwise pay out as a bonus, but it generates a tax deduction for the fair market value of the stock, saving additional cash.
- **Stock grants provide continuing motivation for the recipients to help the company grow.** As with all forms of equity compensation, and unlike a cash bonus, the award of a stock grant puts the

employee in a position to gain further financial benefit if the company increases in value.

New Variations on the Traditional Concept

Performance Shares. Performance shares (or performance units) have become much more prevalent in recent years, especially at publicly traded companies, partly in response to corporate scandals. The premise of such programs is that executives will only be rewarded if corporate performance actually warrants it, and the amount received will be directly proportional to the results achieved. They are also intended to focus executives on key mid-term business objectives that senior management or the board of directors believe are critical to business success.

Performance share programs are based on a performance cycle, typically set at three years. Performance criteria will be set at the beginning of the cycle, usually tied to corporate performance measures ranging from the minimum acceptable to exceptional performance levels. More than one performance measure is often used. So, for example, a plan might set performance targets based both on profitability increases and return on capital. At the end of the performance period, the number of shares delivered to participants will be determined by how the company actually performed on the relevant criteria. Generally speaking, the number of shares delivered will be very minimal if performance is at the minimum level and will rise rapidly (often exponentially) if extraordinary performance is achieved.

Performance cycles often overlap, so that where there is a three year performance cycle, a participant may have three sets of awards "running" at the same time.

Performance share programs are somewhat similar in concept to performance-restricted stock grants except that:

- With performance-restricted grant plans, the shares are issued at the beginning of the performance period, but are unvested. They vest only if and as the performance targets are achieved.
- With performance share plans, the shares are only awarded at the end of the performance period, but are immediately vested. The number of shares awarded is based on the extent to which the performance targets are achieved.

Restricted Stock Units. A Restricted Stock Unit (RSU) award is a promise by the company to issue stock at the time the required vesting period is completed. No shares are delivered until the employee satisfies the vesting schedule. At that time, taxes are netted out prior to making the award of shares, with the employee receiving company stock equal to the net after-tax value of the RSU.

This form of equity compensation was pioneered by Microsoft Corporation in the aftermath of the technology industry "bubble-burst" in 2001. It offers significant advantages, especially to publicly traded companies that distribute company equity broadly throughout their workforces, as is common in the high technology industries. By awarding units instead of traditional restricted stock grants, companies gain a number of advantages, including:

1. Eliminating the problematic question of the 83(b) election (see below) and the administrative and communications burdens associated with it.
2. Facilitating the payment of taxes at vesting with an automatic withholding of shares.
3. Reducing shareholder dilution by not issuing shares that employees will immediately sell to cover their tax costs, and delaying shareholder dilution until the vesting period has been completed.
4. Benefiting from consistent tax treatment and timing internationally.

RSUs are not "property" under Section 83 of the Internal Revenue Code as long as they are an unfunded and unsecured promise to pay money or property in the future.

It is important to note the slightly different tax and cash flow implications for the company with RSUs as compared to restricted stock. With restricted stock, the company receives a tax deduction and the *employee* is responsible for the taxes at the vesting date (assuming no 83(b) election). With RSUs, the *company* is responsible for paying the share equivalent tax amount in dollars to the IRS while still receiving the same tax deduction. Therefore, with RSUs, the tax implications are a "wash" for the company but with a slightly negative cash flow impact.

OTHER STOCK GRANT TECHNIQUES

*   **Career Restricted Stock.** Shares are forfeited if the executive leaves the company prior to retirement.
*   **Career Shares.** Shares received as payment of compensation cannot be sold as long as the executive remains with the company, but shares are not forfeited when the executive leaves the company. Long vesting schedules, perhaps as much as 15 years, are sometimes attached to these shares.
*   **Premium Stock Awards.** Extra shares are awarded if employees elect to be paid in stock rather than cash, typically as part of an annual cash incentive program.

Cash Flow Considerations

Stock grants have cash flow consequences for both employees and employers that must be considered. A stock grant results in a tax liability for the employee, and a payroll tax requirement on the part of the employer (these are discussed further in the next section). To solve the cash flow issues for employees, some companies plan a simultaneous cash bonus to the employee (which is also taxable[1]) to provide ready money for the taxes required on the stock portion of the bonus. Some companies incorporate stock grants into an already-established cash bonus or profit sharing plan. This combination provides the employee with a long-term incentive through stock appreciation, as well a short-term cash incentive through cash profit sharing or bonuses.

Tax and Cost Implications

Tax implications for non-restricted stock bonuses and performance shares are straightforward. For the employee, the fair market value of the stock is taxed as ordinary income on the date the stock is issued to the employee. The company receives a corresponding tax deduction equal to the amount of income the employee must recognize.

The company is responsible for withholding employment taxes from the employee. This must be done by a lump-sum withholding at the time of the award. Generally speaking, withholdings on such awards are determined on a flat rate basis, as opposed to the employee's ordinary tax withholding rate which reflects the individual's personal exemptions and other tax attributes. The current federal withholding rate on supplemental wage payments is 25%. Some states also impose flat rate withholding on these amounts. FICA taxes are also due at the same time. If current pay is not sufficient to satisfy the tax liabilities, the employee may write a check to pay the balance due.

To encourage employees to keep all of the stock, some employers lend employees the money required to pay the tax liability and then withhold a sufficient amount from paychecks during the remainder of the year to pay back the loan. Employers should be careful that the loan is properly structured to avoid the possibility of imputed interest. In addition, public companies may be prevented from granting such loans to their executive officers.[2]

A different set of tax rules applies to restricted stock grants. The employee is not required to recognize any income from the grant until the restrictions have lapsed and the stock is no longer subject to a substantial risk of forfeiture (in other

---

1 Such a cash bonus should be grossed up for the taxes on the bonus, such that the after-tax bonus is equal to the tax liability on the stock award.

2 The Sarbanes-Oxley legislation prohibits personal loans to executive officers. This legislation applies to SEC registrants.

EXAMPLE OF A RESTRICTED STOCK GRANT

Assumptions:

Jack receives a stock grant of 1,000 shares on January 1, Year 1, when the fair market value (FMV)[1] of the stock is $10/share.

The stock value increases 50% per year.

Ordinary income tax rate 28%, capital gains rate 15%.

The stock award vests at 25% per year.

The stock is sold in Year 6 for $75.94/share.

Taxes Paid Year[3]	Without Section 83(b) election	With Section 83(b) election
1	$0	$2,800
2	$1,050[2]	$0
3	$1,575	$0
4	$2,362	$0
5	$3,543	$0
6	$6,820[4]	$9,890
Total Taxes Paid	$15,351	$12,691

1 Fair market value is defined as the price at which an asset (such as a share of stock) would change hands between a willing buyer and a willing seller when the buyer is not under any compulsion to buy and the seller is not under any compulsion to sell, and both parties are able, as well as willing, to trade and are well informed about the asset and the market for that type of asset. Fair market value is always stated as of a specific point in time and may change from day to day, as it does with publicly traded stocks.

2 250 vested shares, multiplied by $15/share (the new FMV of the stock in Year 2) multiplied by the ordinary income tax rate of 28%.

3 Numbers are rounded.

4 Tax on the total proceeds received for the sale less the cost basis of the shares.

words, the vesting requirements have been satisfied). At that point, the employee would have to recognize the then-current value of the stock as ordinary income.

This tax treatment can present quite a problem for the employee who is granted restricted stock that rapidly appreciates in value. For example, an employee who is granted $10,000 in stock that appreciates at 50% per year, and is restricted by a four-year time-based vesting schedule, could be hit with an aggregate tax bill of over $12,000 by the end of the vesting period.

An exception to the rule on restricted stock allows employees to avoid being taxed at ordinary income tax rates on increases in the value of the stock. Under Section 83(b) of the Internal Revenue Code, an employee may file an election within 30 days of the grant that allows him to pay taxes based on the stock value on the date the stock is awarded.[3] If and when the stock eventually becomes

---

3 An 83(b) election is not available for performance shares as the shares are not actually issued until the end of the performance period. Accordingly, the entire value of the stock delivered will be considered ordinary income at that time.

vested, the employee would not have to pay any additional taxes at that time on any gains in the stock value during the vesting period. That increase in value would be taxed at the lower capital gains rate when the stock is eventually sold. Accordingly, a Section 83(b) election converts a portion of what would otherwise be ordinary income into capital gains income, and defers payment of taxes on that income until the employee sells the stock.

Section 83(b) can create some financial risk for employees. If employees forfeit the stock for any reason (such as terminating service before meeting vesting requirements), there will not be a refund of the taxes previously paid. In addition, if the value of the stock decreases after a Section 83(b) election is made, the employee will ultimately have paid more taxes than would have been required had the election not been made and taxes had instead been paid at vesting. This decrease in value will be characterized upon the ultimate sale as a capital loss subject to the capital loss limitation rules.

A Section 83(b) election is most advantageous when there is significant potential for large stock price increases over the vesting period (as in start-up or fast-growth companies) and where an employee is confident of staying with the company through the vesting period.

Stock grants are fairly simple to establish and administer. However, they may be subject to federal and most states' securities legislation, although exemptions are typically available for stock granted to employees. It is important to consult legal counsel to determine whether such exemptions are available, as the penalties for failing to comply with securities laws can be severe. The costs to implement a stock grant program may run $3,000 to $10,000. Typically, administration costs are low, since most plans can be administered internally.

ADVANTAGES AND DRAWBACKS

Advantages
- Stock grants are simple to establish and understand.
- A stock grant puts ownership directly into the hands of the employees.
- They permit flexibility with regard to selection of recipients and size of awards.
- The employer saves cash by paying incentive compensation in stock while also capturing a tax deduction for the current value of the stock grant.
- With a vesting schedule attached, a stock grant can serve as an effective retention tool.

- Stock grants have both "downside risk" and "upside potential," and provide value to employees even during economic downturns.
- The accounting treatment of stock grants is simpler than stock options or discounted stock purchase plans.

Drawbacks

- Since no out-of-pocket cash investment is required, employees may not fully appreciate the ownership value.
- Employees may experience cash-flow problems as a result of the tax consequences of receiving the stock grant.
- Upon vesting, private company employers may need to assist employees in satisfying tax withholdings by repurchasing some shares or otherwise paying additional compensation to employees, which will be a drain on the company's resources.
- Employers must recognize compensation expense for financial accounting purposes.

ACCOUNTING CONSIDERATIONS

Generally, the compensation expense that must be accounted for is the market value of the stock at grant. This amount is charged to earnings over the restricted period as service-based vesting occurs, and is adjusted for actual forfeitures based on failure to meet the service conditions. However, if vesting is based on one or more performance objectives (as in the case of performance-restricted stock or performance shares), the accounting treatment of the award will vary depending upon the nature of the performance condition.

The value of awards with market-based performance conditions (such as awards that will vest based on increases in stock price or stock performance against an index) will have their calculated value reduced to reflect these conditions and the resulting cost will be reflected over the service period, which is typically determined by analysis of when it is likely that the performance condition will be achieved.

Earnings per share are diluted when vested stock is granted, since this involves the issuance of actual shares. Restricted stock grants are generally considered to be common stock equivalents and are therefore factored into certain determinations of earnings per share.

Pros and Cons of the 83(b) Election

Advantages of the 83(b) Election

- Even if the stock increases in value during the vesting period, the employee, having paid income tax at ordinary rates on the full value of the stock at grant, will not have any further income tax to pay when and as the restrictions lapse, nor will the company need to provide any assistance to the employee in connection with the payment of income tax when the vesting restriction lapses.
- When the employee eventually sells the stock, all of the increase in value from the grant date will be taxed at the lower capital gains rate rather than being taxed at least in part at ordinary income tax rates.
- The one-year holding period for capital gains treatment begins in the year the 83(b) election is made.
- The company is entitled to a deduction at the same time and in the same amount as the employee recognizes income.

Disadvantages of the 83(b) Election

- If the stock is forfeited, there is no refund, tax credit or deduction allowed for the tax already paid.
- The tax liability is immediate, rather than deferred, and since the stock is unvested, the employee will generally be required to fund the taxes out of personal resources.
- A reduction in the value of the stock grant over the restricted period will result in an overpayment of taxes.

Tax of 15% on the total proceeds received for the sale less the cost basis of the shares. In the case of restricted stock, the cost basis is the amount included in income, either as it vests, or pursuant to a Section 83(b) election.

Chapter Three

Non-Qualified Stock
Purchase Programs

S tock purchase programs provide employees with the opportunity
to participate as owners by investing in the stock of their employer.
These programs are popular with employers for a number of reasons, including:

- **Avoidance of dilution.** A company's current owners are likely to feel
  much more comfortable about letting employees become shareholders if the owners don't have to "give it away."
- **Cash flow benefits.** Employees who purchase stock are putting cash
  into the company.
- **Simplicity.** An employee purchase of stock at fair market value is a
  very simple transaction from a tax, accounting and recordkeeping
  perspective.
- **Employee commitment.** Many company managers believe that
  stock ownership is more meaningful and that employees will take it
  more seriously if they have invested their own money. Certainly, it
  is likely to be the case that if employees are given a choice to invest
  or not, only those who are seriously committed to helping build the
  company's future will make the choice to put their money into a purchase of stock.

Employee stock purchase arrangements may be broadly divided into two
forms: qualified plans and non-qualified plans. The term "non-qualified" simply
refers to the fact that the purchase program does not follow a particular set of
operating rules that are set out in Section 423 of the Internal Revenue Code, and
therefore does not qualify for the special tax treatment that is available if those
prescribed rules are followed. The tax treatment for non-qualified plans is not

particularly onerous, and compliance with the qualification rules is entirely optional. As a practical matter, the qualification rules are impractical for most privately held companies to follow, so qualified employee stock purchase plans (commonly known as ESPPs or 423 plans) are primarily the domain of publicly traded companies. This chapter addresses non-qualified stock purchase programs. Qualified stock purchase plans are discussed in Chapter Five.

HOW THEY WORK

Non-qualified stock purchase plans are very flexible and can be tailored to a single employee, a select group of employees, or made available company-wide. A non-qualified stock purchase arrangement is simply an offer made to one or more employees to sell them a specified number of shares of stock. In some circumstances, a company may make a loan to employees to finance their purchases, which the employees repay over time.[4] Companies may encourage employee purchase of company stock by offering the stock at a discounted price or by offering to match a purchase of stock with an award of additional equity, often in the form of stock options, to make the purchase offer more attractive to employees.

Because variations in designing direct stock purchase plans are almost limitless, these plans can be tailored to address the particular financial, tax and other strategic needs of the company and its employees. Examples of frequently seen purchase programs include:

- **Purchase Plans for Start-ups.** To foster commitment and to allow potential stock gains to be eligible for capital gains tax treatment, many companies in the start-up phase will give employees the opportunity to purchase shares of common stock in the company. Because of the risk involved in start-up companies and because common stock typically has lesser dividend preference and liquidation rights compared to preferred stock, common shares are usually valued at a comparatively lower price. In virtually all cases, vesting schedules are attached to the shares, requiring the employee to stay with the company for a number of years (typically three to five) to benefit from the appreciation of the stock. If the employee terminates employment prior to vesting in the stock, the plan would provide for the company to purchase those shares back from the employee at the price the employee paid.

  If the stock is subject to vesting, it is extremely important that the employee be aware of the opportunity to file a Section 83(b) election

---

4 Public companies are prohibited from making loans to executive officers under the Sarbanes-Oxley legislation.

(see Chapter Two), ensuring that any future appreciation in the shares will not be taxable until they are sold. For many early stage start-up companies, particularly those intending to do an initial public offering (IPO), stock purchase plans can be preferable to stock option plans because direct purchases at low start-up valuation levels can eliminate potential problems associated with the alternative minimum tax (AMT).[5] In addition, assuming the stock is held for more than one year and a Section 83(b) election is made for restricted shares, the entire gain on the sale is taxed at favorable capital gains rates.

- **Discounted Stock Purchases.** Companies may offer employees the ability to purchase stock at a discount, sometimes with conditions attached such as restrictions on transfer or the required purchase of additional stock. This provides an incentive for key employees to purchase stock in the company, thus gaining employee buy-in and commitment to the long-term growth of the organization. Be aware, however, that the amount of discount from a stock's established fair market value is considered to be current income to the employee for tax purposes (see the section on "Tax Implications" below).

- **Matching Awards.** As an alternative to offering a price discount to buyers, a company can promote employee investment by offering to match any employee purchases with grants of additional shares or stock options. These matching awards would be subject to vesting requirements.

PAY TO PLAY

A major trend occurring in both public and private companies is the requirement that senior executives have a significant investment in the company. A company may require its executives to own a specified amount of the company's stock, the amount of which may be expressed as a multiple of annual salary or a specific number of shares of company stock, with higher ownership requirements corresponding to increased job responsibility. These plans are sometimes called Executive Targeted Ownership Programs (ETOPs).

SECURITIES LAW REQUIREMENTS

Any time a company offers stock for sale to employees, federal and state securities laws must be carefully considered. The securities laws provide that a company must register with the Securities and Exchange Commission (SEC)

---

5 For more details on stock options and the impact of AMT, see Chapter Four.

before it may sell its stock to anyone, unless the proposed sale of stock qualifies for an exemption from the registration process. The registration process is prohibitively expensive for most privately held companies. Fortunately the securities laws provide a number of exemptions that usually make it possible for a private company to carry out an employee stock purchase program (See Chapter Eleven for a discussion of these exemptions). Be aware, however, that the securities laws are complex and violating them can be quite serious. For this reason, a qualified securities attorney should be consulted before undertaking a sale of stock to employees.

TAX IMPLICATIONS

The tax treatment of non-qualified stock purchase plans is generally quite straightforward. The value of any price discount or matching grant of additional shares will result in ordinary income to the employee based on the difference between fair market value at the date of purchase and the purchase price. However, absent a Section 83(b) election, if the stock is not vested at the time of purchase, the value of the stock (less what the employee paid) will be included in income on the vesting date. (See Chapter Two for a discussion of the taxation of restricted stock.) The employer receives a corresponding tax deduction when the employee realizes the income.

Section 1202 of the Internal Revenue Code makes individuals (including employees) who acquire stock in a qualifying small business eligible for a reduced capital gains rate of 7.5% for qualifying stock sales. To qualify, the stock must be held for at least five years.

SET-UP COSTS

A non-qualified stock purchase plan is one of the most inexpensive employee ownership plans to implement. Costs can run as low as $2,000 to $5,000. The primary cost is the attorney's fee for reviewing applicable securities law restrictions and exemptions and developing a shareholder agreement that will control the sale of company stock to outsiders and specify any other conditions on the shares purchased by the employees.

Capital Gains Reduction for Small Business Stock (Section 1202)

The following requirements must be met in order to be considered a qualified small business stock for the purposes of Section 1202:

- Issuing company must be a C Corporation.
- "Active" business requirement must be satisfied.
- Stock must be originally issued after August 10, 1993.
- Stock must be acquired by the taxpayer at its original issue in exchange for money or property (not including exchanged stock), or as compensation for services provided to the issuing corporation.

A qualified small business is any trade or business other than:

- A trade or business involved in the performance of services in the field of health, law, engineering, architecture, accounting, actuarial services, brokerage services, or any trade or business where the principal assets are the reputation or skill of one or more of its employees.
- A banking, insurance, financing, leasing, investing or similar business.
- A farming business.
- A business involving the production or extraction of products that allow for the depletion deduction (mining).
- A business of operating a hotel, motel, restaurant or similar enterprise.

Additionally, the corporation must meet a gross asset test in order to be considered a "qualifying small business." The gross asset test is satisfied if the corporation's aggregate gross assets do not exceed $50 million at any time after August 10, 1993 and before the issuance of the shares. In addition, the aggregate gross assets of the corporation must not exceed $50 million immediately after the issuance of the shares, including any amounts received by the corporation due to the issuance of the shares. Once the shares are issued, they will continue to be considered qualified small business stock even if the corporation's assets exceed the $50 million threshold, although this would prevent the corporation from being treated as a qualified small business regarding future issuance of shares.

ADVANTAGES AND DRAWBACKS

Advantages
- Stock ownership is generally considered to be more meaningful to employees who have invested their own funds to acquire the shares.
- Direct stock purchases can be particularly advantageous for start-up companies looking to save cash while still offering employees significant compensation incentives.
- Employees become investors in the company and thus become more aligned with the goals and objectives of non-employee shareholders.
- Stock purchase plans can generate a modest amount of capital for the company.

Drawbacks
- Employees may be unwilling or even unable to provide cash or agree to a payroll reduction to invest in the company.
- If shares are not immediately vested, employees need to be educated concerning the tax consequences of the arrangement, and must determine whether to make an 83(b) election.
- For private companies, it is advisable to establish contractual restrictions on the transferability of shares and to make provision for future liquidity of the employees' investments.

ACCOUNTING CONSIDERATIONS

Employee purchases of company stock will generally not be accounted for as a compensatory arrangement if shares are sold to employees at fair market value and on the same terms and conditions applicable to all other holders of that class of shares. If these conditions are not met, a non-qualified stock purchase plan may be considered compensatory which will result in an accounting charge to earnings. It may be possible to justify a small discount from fair market value without the program being considered compensatory. A discount of up to 5% is permissible under a safe-harbor exception. A discount in excess of 5% may be justified if it is determined that this amount does not exceed what the share issuance costs would have been if a significant amount of capital was raised in a public offering.

Chapter Four

Stock Option Plans

During the technology boom days of the late 1990s, stock options became by far the most widely used means of giving employees a stake in the equity of a company. The great popularity of stock options during this period was due to several factors. Employers found them attractive because:

- Option plans were simple and inexpensive to create.
- They offered great flexibility, with few restrictive regulations.
- They were not considered compensation expense, improving the appearance of the company's financial statements.
- In many situations, they could be offered in lieu of cash as a form of employee compensation, positively affecting corporate cash flow.
- They provided a well-structured incentive for employees, who would benefit only if, and to the extent that, a company increased its market value—an arrangement that worked well in an economic environment in which market values could often climb quickly and steeply.

Likewise, employees found stock options attractive because:

- They required no up-front investment.
- They produced no up-front tax liability.
- They had heard the stories of other employees getting rich through stock options.

Since those heady days, much has changed, most substantially the effect of options on a company's income statement. While stock options can no longer be turned to as the default choice for employee ownership, in the right circumstances options remain an effective equity-sharing tool.

Companies of all sizes use stock options to provide incentives for individual employees. Options are particularly valuable for smaller companies or start-ups that want to use stock as a form of compensation while preserving cash during the early stages of the company's growth. In addition, companies use stock options to recruit, retain and motivate their workforce. At any stage of a company's growth, stock options can help align employee interests with those of other shareholders because employees have the opportunity to participate in any increased value they help generate. The exercise of options can also bring capital into the company.

HOW THEY WORK

In a stock option plan, company management determines who is eligible to receive options and in what quantity. The company's board of directors (or the board compensation committee) then acts upon management's recommendations. Employees who receive options have a contractual right, or option, to buy a certain number of the company's shares during a specific time period (known as the term or life of the option), paying a price that is specified at the time of grant (known as the exercise price). The life of an option is typically in the range of 5 to 10 years. The exercise price is almost universally set at the stock's fair market value on the date the option is granted. The concept behind options is that if the value of the company's stock goes up in the years following the grant, the employee can benefit by being allowed to purchase the stock at a lower price. If, on the other hand, the value of the stock decreases from the date the option is granted, the employee is under no obligation to purchase the shares.

An example illustrates these concepts:

- Acme Company issues Joe an option allowing him to purchase 100 shares of Acme's stock at the current price of $1 per share (which is also the exercise price).

- The option term is 10 years, meaning that Joe has 10 years from the date the option is issued to him in which to exercise the option (that is, pay for the stock at the specified price).

- If during the term of the option, Acme's stock price has increased to $5 per share, Joe can exercise his right under the option of paying $100, and receiving shares worth $500.

- If, on the other hand, the price decreases after the option is granted, Joe would forgo exercising the option, thereby suffering no out-of-pocket financial loss.

Stock options typically require employees to pay the exercise price in cash and to pay any withholding taxes due on the option gain at the time the option is exercised. The employer may perceive this cash outlay as a positive (a personal investment in the company by employees) while employees may perceive this as a negative (if they cannot afford it or are risk-averse). To reduce or eliminate the cash outlay by employees, many companies allow employees to exercise their options through a "stock-for-stock" transaction or a "cashless exercise." Some companies also permit selected employees to borrow money from the company (typically secured by the purchased stock) to pay the exercise price.[6]

Stock-for-stock transactions enable employees to pay the exercise price (and, in some cases, required withholding taxes) with stock they already own. However the shares used to exercise the option must be owned for at least six months in order to be used to cover the exercise price and still receive favorable tax and accounting treatment. In cashless exercise programs (typically used only by public companies), the employee borrows money from a broker to exercise the option and immediately sells some of the shares to pay back the loan plus any taxes and commissions. Using cashless exercises or stock-for-stock transactions, the employee ends up holding shares representing the value of the spread between the exercise price and the fair market value at the date of exercise, less any taxes paid on the transaction.

INCENTIVE STOCK OPTIONS AND NON-QUALIFIED STOCK OPTIONS

While there is just one set of laws by which stock options operate, there are two possible tax treatments available for stock options, depending on whether or not they comply with the terms and conditions set forth in Section 422 of the Internal Revenue Code.

Compliance with these terms and conditions is entirely up to the company that issues the options. There are no draconian penalties for issuing stock options that do not meet the terms of Code Section 422. There are, however, differences in taxation that will apply to both the employee and the company.

Options that meet the terms of Code Section 422 are known as incentive stock options (ISOs). Options that do not meet the terms of Code Section 422 are known as non-qualified stock options (NSOs). In general, the tax treatment of ISOs can offer significant tax advantages to the employee compared to NSOs. Conversely, NSOs offer more attractive tax terms for the company and provide greater flexibility in terms of plan design since the limitations prescribed in Code Section 422 can be disregarded.

Because NSOs are less tax-advantaged, there are no design requirements imposed on them by the Internal Revenue Code, although certain design limitations may be imposed by state securities requirements. In many cases, the

---

6 Public companies are generally prohibited from making loans to their executive officers under the Sarbanes-Oxley legislation.

Example of a Stock-for-Stock Transaction

Assumptions

- Sue exercises 100 non-qualified stock options with an exercise price of $10/share when the fair market value at the date of exercise is $20/share.
- Sue already owns 200 shares of company stock and uses 50 of them to exercise the option. Her basis of the shares used to exercise the option is $2/share each, or $100 in total.
- She will pay the applicable taxes from the newly acquired shares.
- Combined federal, state and FICA withholding tax rate is 42%.

Number of Optioned Shares to be Exercised	100	(A)
Option Exercise Price	$10/share	(B)
Option Cost (A x B)	$1,000	(C)
Current Stock Price	$20/share	(D)
Number of Shares to be Exchanged (C/D)	50	(E)
Net Newly Acquired Shares (A-E)	50	(F)
Gross Value of Shares Acquired (A x D)	$2,000	(G)
Net Option Gain (G-C)	$1,000	(H)
Applicable Tax (H x 42%)	$420	(I)
Shares Sold to Pay Taxes (I/D)	21	(J)
Total Remaining Shares Sue Receives (F-J)	29	(K)
Basis of Additional Shares (H/F)	$20/share	(L)

In a stock-for-stock transaction, no recognition of taxable income is required since the shares exchanged are considered "like kind." The replacement shares carry the tax basis and acquisition date of the original shares turned in. Newly acquired shares have a basis equal to the taxable income (spread) recognized on the exchange. The shares sold or withheld by the company to pay taxes are considered to be from the newly acquired shares but do not create taxable income because the sales price is equal to the basis.

> ## Summary of ISO Requirements
>
> - The option price cannot be less than 100% of fair market value on the grant date.
> - The aggregate face value of options that may first become exercisable by any one individual in any one year is limited to $100,000, measured as of the date of grant.
> - For shareholders owning 10% or more of voting stock, the option price may not be less than 110% of fair market value on date of grant.
> - To receive favorable tax treatment, employees must hold shares acquired through an ISO for at least two years after the option grant date and one year after the exercise date.
> - ISOs must be granted under a written plan approved by shareholders within 12 months of the plan being adopted. The governing plan must have a term of not more than 10 years from the date of adoption.
> - The plan must specify the total number of shares that may be issued and the class of employees eligible for option grants.
> - ISOs may be granted only to employees (not consultants or non-employee directors).

terms of NSOs are identical to ISOs, and the governing plan document would meet all the requirements specified above. However, in order to have NSO tax treatment, the plan document and award agreements should specify that the stock option is intended to be an NSO. ISOs that are exercised and sold prior to the end of the required holding period are generally taxed similarly to NSOs.

TAX AND COST IMPLICATIONS

Under either an ISO or an NSO plan, there is no tax consequence to the employer or the employee at the time options are granted to employees.

However, the tax treatment that occurs at the exercise date and disposition (sale) date differs, depending upon whether the option is an ISO or an NSO.

With an NSO, the employee must generally pay ordinary income tax on the difference between the exercise price and the value of the stock on the date the option is exercised (when the stock is purchased). The company can claim a corresponding tax deduction as a compensation expense. Upon sale of the stock, the employee must pay capital gains tax on the difference between the stock price

---

NEW RULES DISCOURAGE DISCOUNTED STOCK OPTIONS

Under new tax rules governing deferred compensation plans, options that are issued at a discount to the fair market value of the stock on the date of grant are treated as deferred compensation plans, and the employee will become subject to tax on the deferred compensation[1] on the date of vesting, plus a 20% penalty and interest. Accordingly, discounted options will become very rare in practice, and companies should make reasonable efforts to determine an appropriate value for the stock when options are being granted.

---

1 In the case of an option issued at a discount to fair market value, it is not clear whether only the amount of the discount or the entire accrued gain would be required to be included in income.

---

on the exercise date and the sale price. If the value declines between the exercise date and the date of sale, the loss will be treated as a capital loss.

With an ISO, the employee does not recognize taxable income upon exercise (nor does the employer recognize a deductible compensation expense). Instead, tax liability is incurred only when the stock is sold (or disposed of by other kinds of transfers, such as gifts). If the employee holds the shares acquired through the exercise of the ISO until at least one year has passed (and two years have passed since the date the option was granted to him), the gain realized on a sale of the shares will be reported as a long-term capital gain and taxed only at capital gains rates. The gain will be calculated based on the difference between the proceeds on the sale and the price paid at exercise. The gain at the exercise date may, however, cause the employee to owe federal alternative minimum tax (AMT). If an employee exercises an ISO but does not hold the resulting stock for the required time period specified above, the tax consequences for the employee will be the same as if the option was an NSO.

With an ISO, the company does not receive a deduction unless the employee fails to hold the stock for the period required to receive tax favored treatment—two years from grant and one year from exercise. In such a case, the corporate tax deduction is typically equal to the gain at the exercise date, calculated as the difference between the price paid and the fair market value at the exercise date.[7] The employee must report this income on his tax return as ordinary income, but no withholding taxes are due at the time of sale. If the employer is aware of this disqualifying disposition, it should also report the gain on the employee's

---

7 Where the employee has failed to meet the holding period and where the stock price has declined between the time of exercise and the time of sale, the employee is only required to recognize the net gain as ordinary income, instead of an ordinary income gain and an offsetting capital loss.

annual W-2 form. It is important that the company set up a system for tracking the holding period of stock acquired through the exercise of an ISO.

Option Plan Costs

Stock option plans are relatively inexpensive to establish and maintain. Legal fees to establish the plan can run as low as $3,000 to $5,000 for a small private company. Administrative costs typically remain low, depending on the complexity of the plan, the number of optionees, whether or not the company is required to register its stock, and whether the company outsources the administrative responsibilities or handles them internally. Corporations may initially need outside assistance to determine the cost of options for accounting purposes.

WHEN TO USE AN ISO VERSUS AN NSO

Determining which route is more advantageous—ISO or NSO—is a complex question that will likely depend on the circumstances and priorities of each company. A number of factors should be considered.

While NSOs offer more flexibility of design, ISOs can provide tax savings to employees because of the deferral of taxation and the conversion of ordinary income to a capital gain. The deferral of tax can often result in employees holding more shares post-exercise than would be the case with NSOs where tax withholdings are due on exercise. However, the disadvantages of ISOs—potential AMT exposure for employees and the lack of a tax deduction for employers—must be considered in determining which plan design to use. ISOs are also somewhat more difficult than NSOs to administer and to explain to employees. Careful analysis of the tradeoffs on employee and employer tax implications should be done before choosing which type of plan to implement.

From an income tax perspective, ISOs will be more valuable to employees as the difference between ordinary and capital gains tax rates increases. The drawback for the company is that with an ISO, the employer does not receive a tax deduction. For companies that do not expect to have taxable income during the period in which the stock options will likely be exercised, it may be more advantageous overall to issue ISOs. This is because the company tax deduction available with NSOs is worth less when the company is not profitable, although deductions may be carried forward to profitable years.

The potential exposure of employees to AMT can generate very unfavorable employee relations, and is very difficult to predict in advance, as the liability for AMT depends on many employee-specific factors that are typically not known to employers. It is possible to permit employees to exercise ISOs early, which allows them to take ownership of the stock when the gain may be smaller. Employees can then limit their exposure to AMT by making a Section 83(b) election (discussed in

Illustration of Tax Implications of ISOs Versus NSOs

Assumptions:
- Mary receives 200 options.
- Grant price of $10/share (FMV).
- Option term is 5 years.
- Stock price is $15/share in year 5 when Mary exercises.
- Stock price is $20/share in year 10 when Mary sells.

At Grant Date	ISO	NSO
For Company	No deduction	No deduction
For Mary	No taxable income	No taxable income
At exercise date (year 5):		
Mary pays $2,000 to exercise options on shares worth $3,000	She recognizes no taxable income for regular tax purposes (AMT liability possible)	She recognizes $1,000 ordinary income on difference between exercise price ($2,000) and current FMV $3,000) Withholdings for taxes and FICA are due on exercise
Company receives $2,000 when option for 200 shares is exercised	Company cannot claim any tax deduction	Company can claim tax deduction of $1,000
At disposition (year 10):		
Mary sells 200 shares for $20/share or $4,000 ($2,000) on difference between exercise price ($2,000) and sale price ($4,000)	She recognizes long-term capital gain income ($1,000) on difference between FMV at exercise ($3,000) and sale price ($4,000)	She recognizes long-term capital gain income

Chapter Two).[8] Even if employers want to use ISOs, the limitation on the number of ISOs that can be issued to an employee within a 12 month period may in effect force the employer to grant NSOs for the excess.

In fast-growth companies whose stock value may increase significantly over

---

8 However, this early exercise does not start the clock running for purposes of determining whether the employee has held the ISO shares for the requisite holding period.

the option period, the employee may not be able to afford to pay the exercise price and the tax on the appreciation due upon exercise of an NSO. This is particularly true in private companies that do not have a ready market for their shares.

OPTION EXERCISE

Because option exercise creates a tax liability for employees, they are typically required to deposit sufficient funds to satisfy any required withholding taxes prior to exercising the options. However, there are a number of ways that companies address the potentially negative cash-flow implications for employees that may result from the exercise of non-qualified stock options. In some cases, the company will repurchase sufficient shares to fund the tax obligation.

- Some companies are willing to share with employees a portion of the benefits received from the company's tax deduction by providing a "bonus gross-up" (a cash bonus that the employee can use to pay taxes upon exercise). This can be more valuable to the employee than the tax savings from an ISO.
- Employees may be permitted to pay the exercise price and associated taxes with stock already owned, thereby limiting the employee's required cash outlay at the time the option is exercised. In this stock-for-stock transaction, stock withheld for tax purposes can only cover the employer's minimum statutory withholding requirements. Any excess withholding may cause the plan to be viewed as a liability instead of an equity award for accounting purposes which will generally increase the accounting expense to be charged to earnings.
- As previously mentioned, public companies typically let employees exercise their options using a "cashless" method, which allows employees to borrow funds from the broker to pay the exercise price, taxes and commissions. The employee then immediately sells shares to pay off the loan.

Options generally may not be exercised until they become vested, but some companies add an early-exercise provision to their option grant policies to give employees more flexibility in managing their option grants. An early-exercise program allows employees to exercise their stock options immediately after grant rather than waiting for the completion of any vesting period. The stock purchased is then "restricted" in that the employee would be required to sell it back to the company at the employee's original purchase price if employment terminates before the vesting period is completed. The employee must file a Section 83(b) election, the result of which will vary depending on whether the option is an ISO or an NSO. If the option is an NSO, once the conditions for vesting have been met, the employee attains full ownership rights to the stock and pays no taxes until the shares are sold. If the option is an ISO, an immediate 83(b) election will prevent any exposure to AMT, but long-term capital gains treatment is conditional upon the employee holding the shares for the minimum holding period.

STOCK OPTION PLAN DESIGN CONSIDERATIONS

- **Tie to Business Objectives:** Stock option plans should reinforce business objectives. Depending upon a company's goals for the program, options may be used to reward performance, provide incentives for future performance (such as specific objectives, team performance, or market thrusts), match employee stock purchases, recruit and retain key performers, etc.

- **Vesting:** Companies typically attach a vesting schedule to stock option awards. Vesting schedules are usually time-based, which require the employee to stay with the company for a number of years in order to gain a permanent right to the option and the underlying stock. Annual stock option awards with vesting schedules can be excellent tools for employee retention because employees will always have a portion of several years' worth of unvested option awards that would be forfeited if they terminated employment. Vesting can also be tied to the achievement of performance objectives.

- **Length of Option Term:** An option term is the period of time during which an employee may exercise his options. ISO plans are required to have an option term no longer than 10 years. Most options, whether they are ISOs or NSOs, have a 10-year term, although companies may grant options with shorter periods to encourage employees to exercise the options. Shorter option terms reduce the amount of option "overhang," which is the number of options a company has outstanding at any given time.

- **Pricing:** Most stock option plans specify (and ISO plans require) that the exercise price be set at the fair market value of the stock on the date the option is granted. This is based on the idea that the employees should, and will, share in the increase in stock value that occurs following the grant of the option. A company may discount the exercise price, but this is not a normal practice and would require the company to report any such discount as an expense on its books. For the employee, a significant discount may be treated as a taxable bonus.

- **Size of Awards:** The determination of the overall pool of options to make available to employees should be based on a number of factors including the number of employees that will participate in the plan, the competitive job market, the stage of the company in its development, dilution tolerance by current owners, the company's prospects

UNDERWATER OPTIONS

If, after a stock option has been issued, the value of the underlying stock falls significantly below the exercise price, the option is referred to as being "underwater." Companies can deal with options that are significantly underwater in several different ways:

- **Do nothing.** In this case, the company presumes that the value of the stock will recover sometime over the life of the option term. Employees must be educated accordingly. This strategy risks losing the incentive value of the options if employees feel that the prospect for a stock price rebound is not realistic.

- **Reprice the options.** This means exchanging lower-priced options for the underwater options or amending the terms of the existing options to lower the exercise price. Non-employee investors are generally opposed to repricing because it gives employees a benefit not available to other shareholders. An incremental accounting cost will generally need to be reflected for the repriced options. Companies opting to re-price their options generally restart vesting schedules and require employees to accept fewer replacement options.

- **Cancel the underwater options and issue new ones.** Waiting six months and one day to issue new options may exempt the company from the requirement of expensing the cost of the options on its books. The downside of this strategy is that employees would benefit from a continued low stock price for the six-month period from the cancellation to the new issue date since their options would be revalued at that time.

for growth and industry practice. In determining how many options to award individual employees, the company must consider whether the award will be large enough to be competitive and meaningful to the employee, while being affordable to the employer and other shareholders.

- **Determining Eligible Recipients:** A critical consideration in granting stock options is determining who will be eligible to receive the grants. Some companies limit grants to a few key executives, while others spread them more broadly among employees. In determining who should receive option grants, companies should consider how broadly they could make awards while still ensuring that the awards are sizable enough to have the desired motivational impact on the recipients. Many companies have established broad-based option plans where virtually all employees, even international employees, receive option grants.

- **Valuation:** Stock options do not require independent outside stock valuations. In the case of companies whose stock is not traded on an established stock exchange, the stock price is generally determined by the board of directors, often using a formula, which eliminates the need to hire independent experts (see Chapter 11 for a detailed discussion of valuation). Because an ISO requires that the option price cannot be less than 100% of fair market value at the date of grant, it is critical that the stock pricing formula reflect fair market value when issuing ISOs.

ADVANTAGES AND DRAWBACKS

Advantages

- The company has complete discretion in determining who receives option awards and how many, and whether the shares are subject to vesting, tied to performance objectives, or conditioned on any other criteria.
- Because options only become valuable if the stock price increases, they tie employee rewards to future company success.
- Stock options require an employee investment, but because the option exercise price is set in advance, employees can plan for the cash outlay required at exercise. In addition, while employees must exercise their options to receive any economic value, the fact that they are not required to do so makes options more attractive to employees than stock purchases.
- When employees invest their own money to purchase stock, they will likely be motivated to positively impact the company's growth and earnings through their own performance.
- Most option plans serve as a retention tool by including a vesting schedule requiring the employee to stay with the company for a number of years before the full award can be exercised.

STOCK OPTION TECHNIQUES

- **Merit Stock Options**—Stock options granted in lieu of salary increases or bonuses. Short vesting schedules are usually attached to these shares, but employers must review the schedules for compliance with overtime wage rules.
- **Reload Stock Options**—The automatic grant of a new stock option to replace shares used to exercise an option in a stock-for-stock transaction. Vesting on the reload option is sometimes conditioned upon holding the stock acquired from the original option. These programs are becoming increasingly rare in practice.
- **Performance Based Options**—Option vesting schedule based on company-specific performance objectives.
- **Indexed Options**—Option exercise price changes each year based on a specific index, such as the Consumer Price Index or the Dow Jones Industrial Average, or a peer group of companies. For the options to have value, the stock price would have to appreciate faster than inflation or the average price of other stocks.
- **Transferable Options**—Used mainly for senior executives. This technique allows employees to transfer the options to family members prior to exercising them, thereby reducing the overall size of their estate subject to tax. Not allowed for ISOs.
- **Premium Priced Options**—Exercise price is set higher than fair market value at date of grant, requiring the stock to increase a specific amount before the options will have any intrinsic value.

Drawbacks
- Due to the complexity of stock options and the tax rules governing them, a comprehensive communications program is required so that employees understand what options mean, how to use them and how their own performance affects the underlying stock value.
- Employees, particularly in private companies where there may be no immediate opportunity for selling shares, may take a negative view of the cash outlay required to exercise their options or pay the taxes.

- Some critics argue that stock options don't really provide employees with ownership since no stock actually transfers to employees upon grant and, particularly in the public company environment, employees may sell the shares for a gain immediately after exercise.
- Stock options may promote a short term outlook on the part of employees, since they must be exercised within a limited number of years, and employees tend to sell—and possibly "get out"—immediately after exercising.
- Incentive stock options (ISOs) may generate alternative minimum tax liabilities for participants.
- Investors and other significant shareholders are increasingly skeptical of aggressive stock option plans in which significant numbers of stock options are granted to employees on an annual basis.
- If the company's stock price drops after options have been issued, the options may be rendered worthless in the eyes of the employees, putting pressure on the management of the company to either reprice or issue additional options to employees who are holding underwater options.

ACCOUNTING CONSIDERATIONS

In the past, one of the reasons for the prevalence of stock options was that they were advantageous from a financial accounting perspective; in most cases they were not required to be listed as an expense on the company's income statement. However, beginning in their first period in their first fiscal year commencing after June 15, 2005 (for public companies) or at the end of their first full fiscal year commencing after December 15, 2005 (for non-public companies), stock options are required to be expensed in the company's income statement.

Many private companies do not prepare their financial statements in accordance with Generally Accepted Accounting Principles (GAAP) because their bankers/investors/owners do not require it. However, private companies anticipating a public offering in the near future or that have investors or other stakeholders who require the company's financial statements be prepared in accordance with GAAP will have to comply with the new accounting rules. All public companies are required to comply with this new accounting standard.

The basic thrust of the new rule is that the fair value of the options measured at their grant date must be reflected as an expense over the relevant service period for such options.

An option's fair value is measured by using an option pricing model, such as the Black-Scholes or Binomial models. These models take into account the following factors:

- Current stock price.
- Volatility of the stock (which for private companies is generally determined by using the historical volatility of similar publicly traded companies, or in the absence of such comparables, the volatility of an industry index).
- Term of the option.
- Dividend yield.
- Expected time of exercise (which may be determined by the option pricing model or used as an input, depending on which model is used).
- Risk free rate of return for the period during which the option is expected to be outstanding.

This fair value is computed at the time of grant, and does not vary as a result of subsequent events, unless the attributes of the option itself are amended. So, for example, if the stock price remained completely flat or declined for the entire option term, the calculated expense would still be reflected in the company's books for those options. However, unexpected forfeitures based on failure to meet service-based vesting conditions can result in a decreased expense.

The service period over which this computed fair value is expensed is generally the vesting period of the option. Accordingly, a shorter vesting period will increase the per year expense reflected, while a longer period will decrease the expense reflected in each year.

Certain types of performance-based options are treated differently than as outlined above. The accounting standards differentiate between market-based performance conditions (such as increases in stock price or performance of stock against an index) and other performance conditions (such as achieving a defined level of profit or ROE).

The calculated fair value of options with a market-based performance condition is decreased reflecting the likelihood of achieving those conditions, and the resulting expense will be reflected over the service period. No change will be made to the accounting expense reflected if the stock options do not ever vest by virtue of failing to meet a market-based performance condition.

In contrast, for options with other types of performance conditions, the value of the award is not discounted to reflect the existence of the condition, but the accounting cost of the awards will be adjusted to reflect actual forfeitures of the awards.

All "in the money"[9] stock options outstanding (vested or unvested) should be included in the computation of common stock equivalents for the purpose of determining earnings per share on a diluted basis.

AN EMERGING ALTERNATIVE

Once the most popular means of sharing ownership with employees, stock option programs have become increasingly problematic. Chief among the difficulties that have detracted from options' popularity are:

- The new accounting complexities associated with stock options as a result of major changes in GAAP.
- The problems that result from the fact that employees must come up with the means to pay the exercise price associated with any option that is granted to them. Difficulties in doing so may significantly decrease employee enthusiasm for the program.
- Relative to public companies, the significant dilution to the company's other stockholders that tends to result from the fact that employees typically net only a fraction of the equity value that is contained in a stock option award because of the practice of immediately selling much or all of the stock that is acquired upon exercise of an option.

As an alternative to stock options, many companies are giving consideration to an equity sharing vehicle known as "stock-settled stock appreciation rights" (SS-SARs). SS-SARs are structured to give employees the same result as if they had been issued NSOs and then later exercised those options, immediately selling enough of the shares acquired to cover their cost of exercising the options. As explained in greater detail in Chapter 9, stock appreciation rights are a contractual promise by the employer to pay the employee at some point in the future a sum that will equal the increase in the value of a hypothetical block of shares of the company's stock. In the case of "stock-settled" SARs, the payment is made not in cash but in company stock.

While the net economic result to the employee is essentially the same, it offers the advantages of:

- Reduced dilution of the company's primary owners, since only the "net" number of shares that would normally be kept by a stock option recipient is ever delivered to that individual in the first place.

---

9 Stock options are considered in the money when the value of the underlying shares is greater than the exercise price.

- The employee is not required to come up with any exercise price. Rather than delivering a gross number of shares to the employee, who then gives up a portion to cover the exercise price, the net value the employee is due under the SS-SAR program is simply awarded to the employee directly.
- Simpler accounting treatment. Rather than requiring the use of complex formulas that may end up having little relationship to the final value of the equity awarded to the employee, SARs are "marked to market" each year based on the increase in the value of the "spread" between the starting value of the company's stock and the value of that stock at year-end.

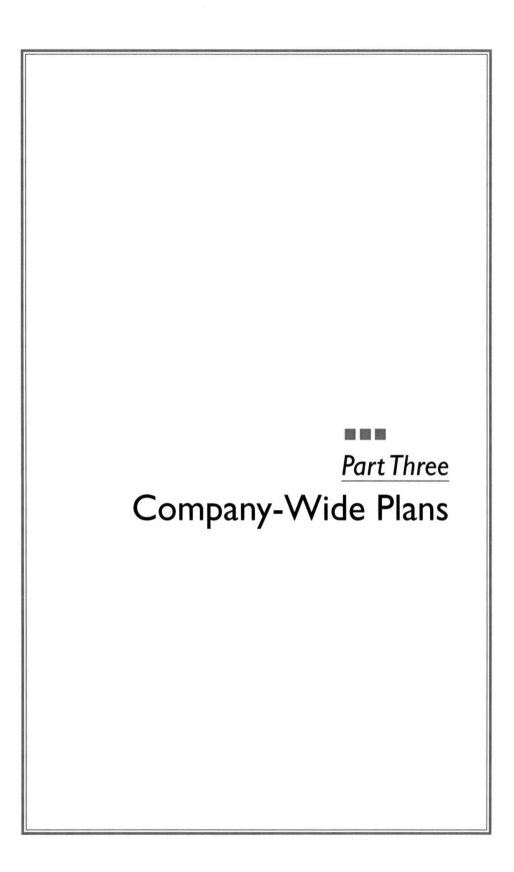

■■■

Part Three

Company-Wide Plans

Chapter Five

Qualified Employee Stock Purchase Plans

Qualified employee stock purchase plans (also known as Section 423 plans or ESPPs) offer employees the chance to purchase company stock at below-market prices. Discounts can be as much as 15%. These plans are best suited to public companies that want to encourage broad-based investment and equity participation.

HOW THEY WORK

ESPPs operate under a set of rules set out in the Internal Revenue Code. These rules allow a company to make its stock available to employees for purchase on advantageous terms. Under the rules, the opportunity to purchase stock must be available to virtually all of the company's full-time employees who have been with the company at least two years. Employees who own 5% or more of the employer's stock are excluded from participating. ESPPs must be approved by shareholders and are only available to current employees.

In these plans, the company typically announces an "offering period" of several months during which employees may defer salary on an after-tax basis through payroll deduction. At the close of the offering period, the plan administrator uses the proceeds from these deferrals to purchase shares for each employee who has elected to participate. These stock purchases are then made at the per-share market price of the stock at the *beginning* of the offering period. This period of delay from the start of the offering period to the date of actual purchase of the shares makes ESPPs similar to incentive stock option plans. Likewise, employee stock purchases through an ESPP are taxed much like purchases made through incentive stock options.

These plans are used primarily by public companies because of the following deterrents for smaller, privately-held companies:

- **Valuation.** Privately held companies would need to develop a methodology for determining ongoing, well-established market values for their shares.

- **Liquidity.** Most employees are reluctant to pay cash for shares that are relatively illiquid, unless a regular internal market is established or an initial public offering or other exit transaction will occur within the foreseeable future.

- **Securities laws.** Securities registration may become necessary for a private company to operate an ESPP. Registration is typically required if a company sells shares to more than 500 shareholders (including employees). Even if the 500-employee limit is not reached, a company would need to comply with the terms of one or more registration exemptions from federal and state securities laws in order to sell stock to employees through an ESPP.

An employee's decision to purchase stock under Section 423 is purely voluntary. Because employees are required to pay for the shares they buy, there will generally not be a high rate of participation by lower-ranking employees. If the plan provides for a reasonably generous discount in the purchase price and the stock's performance has been good, participation by mid- and higher-level employees is generally strong. In the past, companies with ESPPs have experienced participation rates ranging from 30% to 60% of the eligible workforce, but new accounting rules (discussed below) are likely to prompt companies with ESPPs to change the terms of their plans in ways that will make them less attractive to employees. In the face of such changes, rates of participation may drop.

One of the advantages of these programs is that since the shares are purchased with after-tax dollars and do not generate immediate tax liabilities, employees are much more likely to hold shares after their purchase than is the case with stock options.

These plans can make excellent "add-ons" or second plans which, when coupled with another employee ownership vehicle, give those employees who "have the fever" an opportunity to invest further in the company. ESPPs also have the notable advantage of raising capital for the company. Employees who participate in this type of stock purchase plan also immediately become, to the extent of their investment, at-risk investors, thereby increasing their interest in the company's success.

PLAN DESIGN

Key provisions of an ESPP include the offering price (the purchase price of the

How a Qualified ESPP Discount Purchase Works

Assumptions:
- One year stock offering period.
- Purchase price is set at 85% of the lower of fair market value of the stock at the time of grant or at the time the stock is purchased.
- Sam has $850 withheld from his paycheck during the one-year period.

Jan. 1	Dec. 31
Date of Grant	Exercise Date
FMV= $10/share	FMV = $15/share

The plan purchases 10 shares of stock for Sam on Dec. 31 for $8.50/share (85% x $10). Sam gets shares worth $1,500 for $850. The accrued gain per share at the time of purchase is $7.50/share, or 50% of the value of the shares on the date of purchase.

If the share price had declined to $9 on Dec. 31, the plan would have purchased 111 shares at $7.65/share. In this case, Sam gets shares worth $999 for $850, and the accrued gain per share at the time of purchase is $1.35, or 15% of the value of the shares on the date of purchase.

---

stock) and the offering period. Some employers establish the price at fair market value at the date the stock is purchased. Others establish a price that is the lower of the price at the beginning or the end of the offering period, an arrangement known as a "look-back" feature. Legally, either alternative is permissible. Separate and apart from any discount that may result from look-back pricing of stock, a company may also offer employees a pre-set discount, which cannot be more than 15%. Such a pre-set discount guarantees an immediate gain on an employee's stock purchase. If the stock price has risen over the offering period and the plan includes a look-back feature, the built-in gain will be even higher.

TERMS AND CONDITIONS OF ESPPs

A company offering a Section 423 plan is required to extend the right to participate in the program to all employees who meet each of the following stipulations:

- Have been an employee with the company for at least 2 years.
- Work at least 20 hours per week.
- Work a minimum of five months per calendar year.

Employees holding 5% or more of company stock are not eligible to participate.

The maximum length of the offering period for an ESPP depends on whether the company includes a look-back provision in the terms of the program. If no look-back provision is included, the offering period can be up to five years. If a company's program includes a look-back feature, the offering period cannot exceed 27 months. In practice, most companies offering ESPPs have option periods of two years or less; most are set at six months or one year. Note that the new GAAP accounting rules for ESPPs require that companies include their ESPP as an item of compensation expense on their income statements if the plan includes a look-back feature, and the longer the look-back, the greater the potential expense to be recorded. The expense entry for an ESPP, however, is likely to be substantially lower than for a stock option plan, and for either plan, the expense is only a paper entry, not an actual cash cost to the company. Surveys of companies that have offered ESPPs in the past show that few of them plan to drop their program, although some may modify terms of the plan.

There is an annual limit on the number of shares that may be purchased under an ESPP. Specifically, an employee cannot, within a calendar year, purchase stock with a fair market value over $25,000, measured at the *beginning* of the offering period. So for example, the maximum number of shares an employee could purchase if the stock price increased from $10 to $15/share would be 2,500 shares ($25,000/$10). This number does not increase if the stock price declines over the offering period. If the stock price decreased to $9, the employee could still only purchase 2,500 shares, which would have a value of $22,500 on the date of purchase.

SECURITIES LAWS

Because ESPPs involve the sale of corporate securities, securities registration requirements must be carefully analyzed before any sales are made. Failure to meet securities registration requirements or to qualify for registration exemptions could expose the corporate sponsor to severe penalties.

ACCOUNTING IMPLICATIONS

Under accounting standards adopted by FASB[10] and made effective in 2005, most ESPPs are now considered to be compensatory plans, and will have an

---

10 Statement of Financial Accounting Standards No. 123(R), released December 16, 2004.

accounting impact on the employer's earnings for financial statement purposes. This new accounting treatment may lead many companies to modify the terms of their ESPPs. Under the prior rules, corporate sponsors of ESPPs were not required to recognize compensation expense in connection with ESPPs, including any discount on the sale price. Any discount was instead booked as a reduction in shareholder equity.

Under the new rules, any plan with a "look-back" feature or a discount in excess of 5% from the stock price[11] will be considered a compensatory program. While FASB does not mandate a particular method for determining the fair value of ESPP rights, it has indicated that the ESPP should be treated as a combination of a share and a share option. For example, assuming a one-year offering period and an offered 15% discount, the compensation expense would be the sum of the value of .15 of a share and the calculated fair value of an option to acquire .85 of a share with a one-year term.

TAX AND COST IMPLICATIONS

There is no taxable event to the employee at the date of offering or the date the stock is purchased through the ESPP. Instead, the employee must recognize income as of the date the stock is sold. If the price of the stock when it was acquired was less than 100% of the fair market value on the date of purchase (that is, the plan provided a discount), the amount of the discount (measured at the beginning of the offering period for plans with look-back features, and at the time of purchase for all other plans) must be recognized as ordinary income when the stock is sold.[12] The tax basis in the stock is then increased by the income recognized.

The tax due on any additional gain realized at the time of sale will depend on whether the employee has met the required holding period, which is two years from the date the offering period begins and one year after the stock is actually purchased. If the holding period has been met, capital gains tax rates will apply to the difference between the proceeds received on the sale and the new tax basis. If the holding period is not met (a "disqualifying disposition"), the employee is generally required to include as ordinary income the entire gain on the sale of the stock measured from the time of purchase, and the employer is entitled to a corresponding deduction. For this reason, it is important for employers to track disqualifying dispositions by their employees.

Legal costs for establishing an ESPP are relatively modest, typically running less than $10,000 (unless significant securities law compliance work is required).

---

11 Unless a greater discount can be justified based on per share issuance costs if a public offering of shares was made.

12 If the stock has declined in value after purchase but the holding period has been met, the amount to be included in income will not exceed the difference between the proceeds received on the sale and the price paid for the stock.

Most plans are administered by an outside service provider. These annual administration fees generally range from $8 to $15 per employee, usually with a minimum fee that can be as much as $5,000.

ADVANTAGES AND DRAWBACKS

Advantages
- Stock ownership is generally considered to be more meaningful to employees who have invested their own funds to acquire the shares. This is true regardless of the fact that a discount from fair market value is offered.
- Employees have typically already paid for their shares through payroll deductions by the time they actually "purchase" their shares, and the purchase generates no immediate tax liability for the employee. Therefore, employees are under little pressure to immediately sell shares to cover costs, as is typically the case with stock options, and may be more likely to hold their shares for an extended period.
- Programs that offer a discounted price for stock purchases are very attractive to employees and are therefore a great way to get them involved as company shareholders.
- ESPPs are particularly attractive to public companies to facilitate broad-based employee equity investment.
- ESPPs can be attractive to pre-IPO companies because the lower pre-IPO price for employee purchases can be locked in.
- Stock purchase plans generate some capital for the company, although the amounts generated are usually not substantial.

Drawbacks
- Employees with lower levels of compensation may be disinclined to participate.
- Because the tax consequences of ESPPs are somewhat complex, employers will need to develop a good employee communications strategy to support the program.
- For companies that are not publicly traded, the sale of stock to employees may raise significant legal and administrative requirements with respect to compliance with federal and state securities laws, though exemptions may be available.
- Employers will most likely incur an accounting charge for maintaining an ESPP.

Chapter Six

Employee Stock Ownership Plans

Employee Stock Ownership Plans (ESOPs) are tax-qualified, defined contribution plans designed to provide employees with an ownership stake in the company where they work. As tax-qualified retirement plans, ESOPs are subject to the requirements of the Employee Retirement Income Security Act (ERISA) and to the Internal Revenue Code's anti-discrimination provisions.

ESOPs are distinct from other qualified benefit plans in several important respects. Unlike the assets of most defined contribution plans that are invested in a diversified portfolio of stocks and bonds, ESOPs are intended to be invested primarily in the stock of the sponsoring corporation. ESOPs are also unique among qualified plans in that they can borrow money to purchase the sponsoring corporation's stock. This ability to "leverage" the ESOP makes it a compelling corporate finance technique that permits employees to acquire a large ownership stake in their company through a single transaction.

ESOPs also enjoy unique and substantial tax advantages that offer important benefits to the company and its current owners. For C Corporations, these include corporate tax deductions for both principal and interest payments on ESOP loans, a deferral or total avoidance of capital gains taxes for stock sold to an ESOP by owners of privately-held companies, and tax deductions for dividends paid on ESOP stock. ESOPs in S Corporations are entirely exempt from federal income tax.

HOW THEY WORK

Non-leveraged ESOPs

A non-leveraged ESOP is similar to a qualified deferred profit-sharing plan in that the company makes annual contributions to the ESOP trust on behalf of its eligible employees, each of whom has an individual account within the trust. The contribution may be in stock or cash that can be used to purchase stock or to provide the trust with diversified assets. In either case, a C Corporation receives a tax deduction based on the value of the contribution, subject to Internal Revenue Code limitations. The limit on a corporation's tax deduction is 25% of payroll less employer contributions to any other defined contribution plan. The maximum individual salary that may be taken into account for purposes of determining contribution limits was set at $200,000 in 2002, to be adjusted for inflation thereafter in $5,000 increments.

S Corporations receive no tax deduction, but since ESOPs are exempt from federal taxes, the aggregate tax liability is reduced commensurate with the percentage of the company's stock owned by the ESOP.

Corporate contributions are invested primarily in company stock and then allocated to individual employee accounts based on a pre-determined formula, typically one which allocates the stock on a pro-rata basis as an equal percentage of each participant's salary. Employees' accounts grow each year based on company contributions and appreciation of the employer stock in the account, and are paid out to the employee usually upon retirement or termination of employment.

Leveraged ESOPs

A leveraged ESOP is one that borrows money to purchase employer securities for the benefit of the ESOP participants. While funds can be borrowed directly from the sponsoring corporation, usually a bank or other lender loans money to the ESOP or, more typically, to the corporate sponsor which then loans those funds to the ESOP on substantially similar terms. Sometimes stockholders simply sell their stock to the ESOP in exchange for a note. This is referred to as seller-based financing.

Stock purchased by the ESOP trust is initially held in a suspense account and allocated to employees as the ESOP loan is repaid. The corporation makes annual (or more frequent) contributions to the ESOP in an amount at least equal to the ESOP's debt repayment obligation to the lender. Annual corporate contributions are limited to 25% of payroll for purposes of repaying the principal on leveraged ESOP debt. Unlimited interest and "reasonable" dividends may also be used to repay the ESOP loan on a fully tax-deductible basis. In addition, dividends paid

With certain exceptions, ESOPs must satisfy the Internal Revenue Code's requirements applicable to defined contribution plans. Critical issues that should be addressed in plan design include determining:

- Who will participate in the plan.
- How the stock will be allocated to participants.
- What vesting schedule will be used.
- Whether shares held in the ESOP will be voted by a trustee or passed through to the participants.
- How distributions of ESOP accounts will be handled.
- Whether or not to use preferred stock for the ESOP.
- The rights and preferences (if any) of the ESOP stock.

out in cash to participants or reinvested by participants in company stock held within the ESOP are also tax deductible. Contribution limits for S Corporations are 25% of payroll inclusive of interest and contributions to other qualified plans.

As the ESOP loan is repaid, an equivalent portion of the unallocated shares is released from a suspense account and allocated to employee accounts according to a pre-established written formula, usually based on salary, though other non-discriminatory formulas may be used. Because corporate contributions to an ESOP are tax deductible within certain limitations, both the principal and the interest payments on ESOP loans are generally fully tax deductible to the sponsoring C Corporation.

Federal law mandates that an ESOP may pay no more than fair market value for shares it acquires. The creation of an ESOP in a privately held company therefore requires an independent appraisal to determine the fair market value of the stock on at least an annual basis and for all significant transactions involving the ESOP.

ESOP Distributions and the Company's Repurchase Obligation

Employees generally become eligible to receive the vested portion of their account upon the occurrence of certain events such as job termination, retirement, death or disability. For companies whose stock is not publicly traded, the corporation must provide the employees with a market for the shares distributed to them when they leave the ESOP. In most cases, the distribution is made to the employees in cash from funds provided by the company to the ESOP. If the distribution is made in stock, the company is required to repurchase the shares. In either case, the company must prepare for this "repurchase obligation" to mitigate cash-flow problems when distributions are required.

Employees who have attained retirement age (usually defined as 62 or 65) must begin to receive their ESOP benefits within one year after the end of the plan year in which they retire. The corporation may make the payments over a five-year period in annual installments. Employees who terminate service prior to attaining retirement age (or due to disability or death) are generally eligible to start receiving their ESOP distribution five years after the end of the plan year in which they terminated. The company may then spread the payments over an additional five years payable in annual installments. In the case of a leveraged ESOP where a loan is being repaid, a company can delay employee distributions until the loan is paid off in order to preserve cash during the repayment period.

Companies may choose to accelerate ESOP distributions, but all employees must be treated equally. This means that once a distribution schedule has been established, the corporation may not amend the plan's rules to the detriment of the employees' interests. Most closely-held companies therefore adopt a conservative distribution schedule that permits five-year installment payments.

As a practical matter most employees prefer to receive their distributions in cash, but employees generally have a legal right to demand the distribution in stock. In any case, if the distribution is made in stock, the corporation must provide employees with a "put option" on shares distributed to them from the ESOP. This put option obligates the corporation to repurchase the shares within a specified 60-day period in the year following distribution or during a similar period in the next succeeding year. The put option lapses if the participant does not exercise it during either of these two periods. If the stock is "put" to the corporation, the corporation must by law either repurchase the shares directly or enable the ESOP to repurchase those shares subject to the put option. If the ESOP accepts this obligation, it may then use cash in the trust to purchase the shares.

Public company ESOPs typically make a lump-sum distribution of shares to departing participants since employees can simply sell their shares on the stock market. Closely-held companies that are "substantially employee-owned," which is generally interpreted to mean at least 80% ownership by current employees or qualified plans, may require departing ESOP participants to accept cash payments in lieu of company stock. This provision allows employee-owned companies to preserve their employee-owned status over time. S Corporation ESOPs are not required to distribute shares because such distributions could cause the company to become ineligible for S Corporation status.

ESOP Diversification Option

In order to protect those ESOP participants approaching retirement age from undue investment risk, the law requires that such participants be entitled to diversify their holdings in the ESOP. Under the ESOP diversification rules, employees who have reached age 55 and who have 10 years of participation in the ESOP must be given the ability to diversify up to 25% of the shares in their ESOP account. This choice must be made available to eligible employees for a 60-day period during the year in which they become eligible, and again on the same terms each year through age 59. When the employees reach age 60, they must be provided with a final, one-time option to diversify up to 50% of the stock in their accounts. To meet the diversification requirement, employers must provide at least three alternative investment options within the ESOP or another qualified employee benefit plan (typically a 401(k) plan), or the employer can choose to distribute the diversified amount to the employee in cash. If such a cash distribution is rolled over into an IRA, it is not considered to be an early distribution from the plan and is therefore exempt from early withdrawal penalties.

ESOPs AS AN EXIT STRATEGY

For owners of closely held C Corporations, one of the most attractive features of an ESOP is the ability of shareholders to defer capital gains taxes (often permanently) on sales of stock to an ESOP when certain conditions are met. Section 1042 of the Internal Revenue Code provides for what is commonly referred to as the "ESOP Rollover" or "1042 Transaction." This provision is not only an attractive incentive for shareholders of closely-held businesses to transfer part or all of their stock to the employees via an ESOP, but it also offers a potential solution to the often difficult problems of shareholder liquidity and transition to second generation ownership.

Retiring owners or other major shareholders of a privately held company who wish to sell their stock face some potentially unwelcome choices: selling to outside investors, if any are available; exchanging stock with another company in a merger; or selling stock back to the company, if such a transaction is feasible. None of these options is taxed as favorably as a sale to an ESOP which also enables the selling shareholders to diversify their investment on a tax-deferred basis. A sale to an ESOP can also help ensure the company's independent existence.

An ESOP rollover offers tax-advantaged terms to the selling shareholders, establishes a potential market for future sales of stock, helps maintain current employees' jobs and rewards them with an ownership stake. At the same time, it helps retain independence and local ownership of the business. A sale to an ESOP also allows an owner to sell out gradually, withdrawing from the business to whatever extent desired, and can enable a selling shareholder to maintain control over the company during the buyout period.

Under Section 1042, a shareholder or a group of shareholders selling qualified securities to an ESOP in a single transaction incurs no taxable gain on the sale if three principal conditions are met:

- First, the stock sold must be securities of a closely-held C Corporation and the shareholder must have owned the qualified securities for at least three years. Qualified securities do not include stock acquired through stock options, qualified retirement plans, or other compensatory arrangements (unless purchased for fair market value).

- Second, immediately after the sale, the ESOP must hold at least 30% of each class of outstanding stock of the corporation or 30% of the total value of all classes of outstanding stock, including options, issued by the corporation. Once the ESOP obtains a 30% stake, all subsequent sales to the ESOP may also qualify for the Section 1042 tax deferral as long as the ESOP maintains at least a 30% stake.

- Third, within a fifteen-month period that begins three months prior to the date of sale, the seller(s) must purchase qualified replacement property (stocks, bonds or notes of U.S. operating companies) and then file certain information regarding this transaction with that year's personal tax return. If the cost of the replacement property is less than the amount derived from the sale of securities to the ESOP, the difference would be subject to capital gains tax. Proceeds from the sale to the ESOP that are invested in qualified replacement property are deferred from capital gain recognition until the replacement property itself is subsequently sold or transferred. The tax cost basis of the shares sold to the ESOP transfers to the replacement property. If the selling shareholder dies owning the replacement property, the estate will be allowed to step-up the basis of the replacement stock, thereby avoiding capital gains taxes altogether.

Stringent regulations apply to ESOP rollover transactions. For example, family members, direct lineal descendants of the selling shareholder(s) and any shareholders with a stake of 25% or more may not receive allocations of any of the stock for which a seller makes a Section 1042 deferral election. In addition, many lenders require the selling shareholder to pledge part or all of the replacement property as security for the ESOP loan. But if carefully structured, the rollover provision offers entrepreneurs an excellent exit strategy on tax-favored terms while also providing employees with an opportunity to obtain substantial equity in their company.

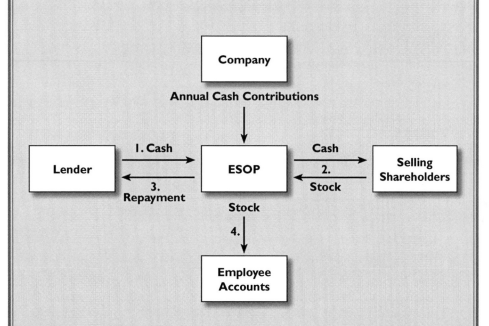

LEVERAGED ESOP PURCHASE OF STOCK FROM SHAREHOLDERS

1. Lender lends money to ESOP with company guarantee.*
2. ESOP uses the money to purchase stock from shareholders.
3. Company makes annual tax deductible contributions to ESOP which in turn are used to repay lender.
4. As the loan is repaid, shares are allocated to employee accounts based on a pre-set formula. Employees receive a distribution when they retire or leave the company.

---

* More typically, the lender will make the loan directly to the company which then makes a "mirror loan" on substantially similar terms to the ESOP. The net corporate tax impact is identical in either scenario.

INNOVATIVE USES OF ESOPs

Facilitate Corporate Divestitures

A common use of leveraged ESOPs is to facilitate corporate divestitures of divisions by using the ESOP to purchase a significant number of shares on behalf of the employees in the divested company. A typical ESOP divestiture transaction would be structured by establishing a new company which would then establish an ESOP. The new company's ESOP would borrow sufficient funds to purchase the division from the parent company. The former parent corporation will typically pay the legal and financial costs associated with the ESOP loan and will sometimes provide a guarantee for the loan and/or retain some equity in the divested company. Lenders usually require the management team to invest personal funds in such a buyout transaction, which can be done through plan-to-plan transfers from accounts that they have in other qualified retirement plans to the new ESOP.

Leveraged Buyout

A leveraged ESOP can also be used to facilitate a buyout of a company by its employees. In such a leveraged buyout, an ESOP loan is used to purchase most or all of the shares of the company. This strategy is used to take a public company private or to purchase substantially all of the shares of a private company.

Finance Investments or Acquisitions

ESOPs can be used to raise the capital needed to finance investments or acquisitions by having the ESOP purchase newly-issued shares from the sponsoring corporation. If the sponsoring corporation simply issues new shares and contributes them to the ESOP, the amount that may be contributed is limited to 25% of covered payroll for that year. It is possible, however, for the corporation to structure a leveraged ESOP loan, backed by a corporate guarantee, to acquire a large block of newly-issued shares to be repaid over several years. The proceeds from that loan can then be used for legitimate corporate purchases such as acquisitions or capital investments. As the loan is repaid, the ESOP participants capture the benefit of that newly-created value as the shares are allocated to their individual accounts. This strategy provides the company with a lower cost financing tool, albeit at the cost of dilution to current shareholders.

Use of Preferred Stock

Federal law requires that ESOPs must own the best common stock issued by the company (ESOPs may not, for example, own non-voting shares). Some companies use a strategy of having the ESOP own convertible preferred stock, which offers several advantages. The primary purpose is to make efficient use of the tax deduction for dividends declared on ESOP stock. The higher dividend rates typically paid to preferred stockholders allow a company to pay down ESOP debt more rapidly through the use of deductible dividends without having to make the same dividend payments on the company's common stock. Similarly, tax-deductible dividends can be paid in cash to ESOP participants (or allocated to their ESOP accounts) as an additional benefit of ownership. An added advantage is that convertible preferred shares carry additional liquidation rights, thereby providing greater security for the ESOP participants and lenders.

ESOP convertible preferred shares are sometimes used in KSOP arrangements as well (a KSOP is a 401(k) plan combined with an ESOP). With this arrangement, dividends on convertible preferred shares purchased or acquired through a corporate match in the employee's 401(k) account are used to provide employees with current income on their savings.

It should be noted that the use of preferred shares is not permitted in an S Corporation since S Corporations may have only one class of stock.

SPECIAL ESOP RULES FOR S CORPORATIONS

ESOP rules for S Corporations differ in several important respects from ESOPs in C Corporations. While both C Corporation ESOPs and S Corporation ESOPs qualify for special tax advantages, these tax incentives are quite distinct.

The primary benefit of being an S Corporation is that the corporation itself pays no federal income tax on its earnings. Instead, the shareholders pay tax on their proportional share of the company's income. This eliminates the potential double taxation which applies to C Corporations (a corporate level tax on profits and an individual shareholder tax on dividend distributions).

An ESOP in an S Corporation is exempt from federal taxes. As a result, to the extent that an ESOP owns shares in an S Corporation, that percentage of the income would not be taxed. To state the obvious, an S Corporation that is 100% owned by an ESOP is entirely exempt from federal income tax. Although most states treat S Corporations the same as the federal government, some consider them to be the same as C Corporations. In these few states, the S Corporation pays state income tax.

To qualify for S Corporation status, a company may have no more than 75 shareholders (the ESOP trustee counts as only one shareholder regardless of the number of participants in the trust) and may issue only one class of stock. An exception to the rule is that there may be voting and nonvoting stock, but no preferred stock. There are also prohibitions on certain types of shareholders. Consequently, neither a nonresident alien nor a C Corporation may own shares in an S Corporation. (Most S Corporations have a shareholders agreement to prevent a stockholder from making a transfer of shares to an impermissible holder which would cause an involuntary termination of the S Corporation status.)

The Section 1042 ESOP deferral is not available to owners of S Corporations for stock sold to an ESOP. However, this election can be made available by having the company convert to C Corporation status. If a company changes to C status, it may not switch back to S status for five years under current IRS requirements. This is frequently acceptable to all concerned because the ESOP loan may have a term of five years or more and the company may not anticipate being in a tax paying position during the debt repayment period.

S Corporations do not qualify for the corporate tax deduction for dividends paid on ESOP shares. In addition, leveraged ESOP interest payments must be included in the 25% limit for annual contributions to the plan for S Corporations.

Section 409(p) Anti-Abuse Provisions

Unfortunately, the tax-exempt status afforded to S Corporation ESOPs has resulted in some unscrupulous transactions that violated the spirit of the law which was intended to benefit employees. In some cases, ESOPs were structured to acquire 100% of an S Corporation to shield the company from taxes for a number of years, but large grants of stock options or other synthetic equity were provided to key employees that, when converted into real equity at a later date, stripped most of the equity value from the ESOP. In other cases, part of an operating company—along with a sizeable portion of the net profits—was transferred to a newly formed S corporation entirely owned by an ESOP which operated free of tax, while funding large deferred compensation plans for a select group of executives with that untaxed income.

As a result, in 2001 Congress changed the tax laws to authorize the Treasury Department to promulgate a new Section 409(p) to regulate S Corporation ESOPs to prevent such abuses. The purpose of Section 409(p) is to limit the tax benefits of ESOPs maintained by S corporations to those in which the ESOP is designed to provide a meaningful benefit to a broad base of rank-and-file employees.

Section 409(p) is essentially an ownership concentration test designed to assure broad-based employee ownership within the ESOP. It requires that if an ESOP holds S Corporation stock, no portion of the ESOP's assets attributable to or allocable in lieu of S Corporation stock may accrue or be allocated for the benefit of any disqualified person under the ESOP or other qualified plan. A plan that does not satisfy this requirement is subject to substantial penalties, as are the individuals having a prohibited allocation.

The Section 409(p) regulations are fairly complex, but essentially a disqualified person is someone who owns more than 10%—either directly or in the form of "synthetic equity"—or whose family owns more than 20% of an ESOP-owned S Corporation. Penalties for violation of the anti-abuse provisions are severe—indeed, draconian—so it is crucial that owners of S Corporations interested in establishing an ESOP consult with a professional tax advisor familiar with these complicated compliance tests.

TAX IMPLICATIONS

ESOPs offer a number of tax advantages to the corporate sponsor, selling shareholders and employees:

- Corporate contributions to ESOPs (whether in cash or stock) are tax deductible up to an annual limit of 25% of payroll.
- For C Corporations, interest payments and "reasonable" dividends used to repay ESOP debt are not subject to the 25% contribution limit.
- Both principal and interest on ESOP loan repayments are tax deductible.
- For C Corporations, dividends declared on ESOP shares are tax deductible if paid in cash to plan participants. These tax deductions must be considered when calculating the corporate alternative minimum tax.
- Shareholders of closely-held companies may defer or even avoid capital gains on the proceeds of sales to an ESOP in a C Corporation if, after the sale, the ESOP owns a minimum of 30% of the company and the seller(s) reinvests the sale proceeds within one year in "qualified replacement property."
- ESOPs in S Corporations are exempt from federal taxes.

The primary tax benefit of an ESOP to employees is the same as it is for all qualified plans in that employer contributions to the trust are tax deferred until the employee actually receives a distribution from the plan.

Another benefit available to employees in ESOPs is that they can reduce their tax payments associated with the distribution of shares from the ESOPs. When stock is distributed directly from the ESOP, the employee is only required to pay taxes on the cost basis of the shares distributed. This is allowed due to the special treatment accorded net unrealized appreciation (NUA) under the tax laws. NUA is the difference between what the trustee(s) of a qualified retirement plan (including an ESOP) pays for the employer securities, and the fair market value of the securities at the time of distribution. Generally, the amount subject to tax in a distribution from a qualified plan, including an ESOP, is the entire fair market value of the distribution, less the value of any employee after-tax contributions. However, if a distribution includes employer securities, all or part of the NUA in the securities is excludable from income. This NUA is not recognized as taxable income until the recipient sells the securities. It is then characterized as a long-term capital gain, regardless of when the sale occurs.

PLAN COSTS

ESOPs are relatively expensive to set up compared to other equity-based plans. Legal fees typically range from $15,000 to $25,000 for non-leveraged plans, and can be significantly higher for complex transactions, particularly those involving leveraged ESOPs. Similar costs will be incurred for an independent appraisal, which must be updated annually. Plan administration can run several thousand dollars annually. Additional costs may be incurred for a feasibility study, trustee fees, bank fees and legal and investment banking assistance. These expenses vary widely, depending upon the size and complexity of the transaction. Leveraged ESOPs for small companies typically cost more than non-leveraged ESOPs, sometimes running to hundreds of thousands of dollars for larger, more complex transactions. Companies who carefully study and implement well planned ESOP strategies can nevertheless qualify for tax benefits greatly in excess of these costs when calculated over the life of the plan.

ADVANTAGES AND DRAWBACKS

Advantages
- ESOPs offer significant tax advantages to the company, employees and selling shareholders.
- ESOPs have a unique ability to borrow money to purchase employer securities to facilitate a variety of corporate finance and ownership transition objectives.
- Employees are able to acquire a large block of stock paid for over time through the future earnings of the corporation rather than from their own savings.
- ESOPs provide the benefits of stock ownership to all participating employees, facilitating corporate efforts to adopt an ownership culture.
- ESOPs offer shareholders of closely-held corporations the ability to sell all or a portion of their ownership to the ESOP on tax-advantaged terms.

- ESOPs enable a transfer of ownership to management and employees as an alternative to a sale to an outside party for business succession or other changes in corporate control.

Drawbacks

- Stock allocations to employees must be made according to a pre-established formula that is normally based on an equal percentage of compensation rather than being based on individual merit.
- Independent appraisal of stock value is required annually for private companies.
- The costs of implementation and administration may be greater than for most other equity compensation plans.
- Closely held companies must repurchase shares from departing participants. This "repurchase obligation" can be substantial for a company whose stock increases in value over time.
- Accounting requirements for leveraged ESOPs can have negative implications for publicly traded companies and private companies required to prepare financial statements in accordance with generally accepted accounting principles.

ACCOUNTING CONSIDERATIONS

Leveraged ESOP debt must be recorded on the balance sheet of the corporate sponsor as a liability. The offsetting entry is a reduction in equity (a contra equity account). In addition, as shares are released from the suspense account, the fair market value of these shares must be taken into account when determining the charge against earnings. This negative accounting treatment makes large leveraged ESOPs challenging for companies that are concerned about their reported earnings and balance sheet presentation. Shares held in the suspense account are not treated as outstanding for the purpose of calculating earnings per share.

■■■■

Part Four

Savings Plans That Can Hold Employer Stock

Chapter Seven

The Use of Stock in 401(k) & Other Qualified Retirement Plans

To encourage retirement savings by employees, the federal government provides tax incentives to corporate sponsors of pension and retirement savings plans. Most of these tax incentives apply to qualified retirement plans. Generally, a qualified retirement plan is a plan in which assets are held in trust for the benefit of employees and paid to the employee at termination of employment or retirement, or to an employee's estate upon the death of the employee. The plans must meet Internal Revenue Code qualification requirements, including anti-discrimination standards, to ensure that the plan benefits are allocated among all participating employees in accordance with approved formulas.

Tax incentives have been instrumental in the popularity of these plans. The corporate sponsor gets a current tax deduction for contributions made to the plan. Employee contributions and appreciation of the plan assets are tax-deferred until distributed to the employee, typically upon termination of service. There are various forms of qualified retirement plans, including defined benefit pension plans, profit sharing plans, money purchase pension plans, ESOPs and 401(k) plans.

In terms of both the total number of plans and plan participants, 401(k) plans are the most popular form of qualified retirement plan in U.S. companies today. Named for the Internal Revenue Code section that spells out its rules and regulations, the 401(k) plan, in its simplest form, is a low-cost method for employers to provide a tax-deferred retirement savings vehicle for employees.

In fact, 401(k) plans have also been one of the most popular qualified plan approaches for providing employees with company stock. When the plan includes employer contributions of company stock to employee accounts and/or allows employee purchases of company stock, it becomes a method for employees to build equity in the company. A 401(k) plan can also be combined with an employee stock ownership plan (ESOP) to form what is sometimes referred to as a KSOP.

HOW THEY WORK

A typical 401(k) plan permits employees to defer a limited amount of compensation into any of several diversified investment options established by the plan's administrative committee. To encourage employee participation in 401(k) plans, corporate sponsors often match employee contributions.

Contributions to 401(k) plans can occur in several different ways. A plan may offer any or all of these features:

- **Employee Deferrals:** The primary rationale for 401(k) plans is to offer employees a means of saving for retirement on a pre-tax basis. Employees elect to have their employer contribute a portion of their compensation into the plan account. The percentage contributed can be as much as 100% of compensation for some employees, subject to the dollar limits and anti-discrimination testing. For income tax purposes, the contribution is considered to be a reduction in the employee's wages and a tax-deductible contribution by the employer. The contribution and any increases in its investment value are exempt from income tax until the assets are distributed to the employee, normally when the employee separates from service with the company. Taxes on the distribution can be further deferred if the employee transfers the assets to another qualified plan or to an individual retirement account (IRA). Employee deferrals are subject to Social Security and Medicare taxes; in most states, other payroll taxes also apply.

- **Employer Matching Contributions:** The second most common feature of 401(k) plans is an employer matching contribution. Matching contributions are often used to encourage lower-paid employees to participate in the plan to help the company meet nondiscrimination requirements, thereby allowing higher paid employees to defer a larger portion of their compensation. The employer contributes an amount that matches employee contributions (usually according to a pre-set formula determined in advance by the employer) that is typically subject to a maximum percentage of the employee's compensation or a maximum dollar amount. For example, an employer may match 50% of the employee's contribution up to a maximum of 6% of an employee's annual compensation. This means that if an employee contributes up to 6% of salary, the company match would be an additional amount equal to 3% of salary. While employee deferrals are always 100% vested, employer matching contributions often include a vesting requirement, which obliges the employee to stay with the company for a specific period of time to qualify for the full benefit of the corporate match. Sometimes, matching contributions are made only for those employees still employed as of the last day of the calendar year, quarter, etc.

- **Employer Discretionary Contribution:** In addition to the matching contribution, employers sometimes elect to make an additional discretionary contribution to the plan. Whereas a matching contribution is provided only to employees who elect to defer a portion of their salary to the plan, an employer discretionary contribution is allocated to all employees who are eligible to participate in the plan. This contribution is commonly referred to as the profit sharing element, whether or not it is directly tied to company profitability. Discretionary contributions are usually allocated to employee accounts, prorated according to compensation level and typically include a vesting requirement. (However, there are allocation methods that can allot more to those who earn over the Social Security taxable wage base, or even assign different percentages to specified groups, subject to IRS anti-discrimination requirements.)

- **Employee After-tax Contributions:** While most 401(k) plans do not permit it, a company may, in limited situations, allow employees to contribute after-tax money to the plan. Though the contribution is included in annual gross income, increases in its investment value are not subject to tax until distribution. This type of contribution is particularly attractive to U.S. taxpayers working abroad whose salaries are wholly or partially exempt from U.S. income tax and who would not qualify for a tax benefit from a salary deferral.

Contribution Limits for 2006 and Beyond

The employee elective deferral limit for 401(k) plans was set at $11,000 in 2002 increasing by $1,000 per year until it reached $15,000 in 2006, to be adjusted for inflation thereafter.

Individuals age 50 or older are allowed to make "catch-up" compensation deferral contributions to a 401(k) plan of up to $5,000 per year in 2006. As a result, an eligible 50 year-old could contribute $20,000 to the plan (the $15,000 limit plus the $5,000 "catch-up"). After 2006, the catch-up contribution is indexed and adjusted for inflation.

401(k) PLANS AND EMPLOYER STOCK

While 401(k) plan assets are typically invested in mutual funds or other diversified investments, they may also be used as a means of providing employees with an opportunity to acquire ownership in their own company. In the simplest approach, all or a portion of the employer matching contribution may be in the form of employer stock. If the stock match is applied uniformly as part of the plan design, it is not considered to be an investment decision on the part of employees to acquire the stock and is therefore generally exempt from securities registration requirements.

Alternatively (or in addition), the plan can be designed to permit employees to invest a portion of their salary deferral in their company's stock. An employee election to invest in company stock is normally subject to securities registration, so this option is usually offered only by publicly traded companies whose stock already meets securities registration requirements. Private companies may also be able to use this option if they qualify for an exemption from federal and state securities registration requirements. SEC Rule 701, for example, provides an exemption from securities registration requirements for companies meeting minimum safe harbor requirements (see Chapter Eleven for a detailed discussion of Rule 701).

It should be noted that a 401(k) plan sponsored by an S Corporation may hold employer securities. However, the income flowing from the S Corporation to the plan will be subject to taxation as "unrelated business taxable income" unless the plan is a KSOP.

SPECIAL 401(k) DISCRIMINATION TESTS AND SAFE HARBOR PROVISIONS

To obtain the tax benefits associated with 401(k) plans, the company sponsor must structure the plan provisions to meet federally mandated anti-discrimination requirements. The requirements are generally established to ensure that these plans benefit a broad cross-section of employees instead of just senior executives or other highly-paid employees. Although all qualified plans must meet anti-discrimination requirements, 401(k) plans must meet additional tests to ensure that there is broad participation among employees at various compensation levels within the company.

The Internal Revenue Service Code provides safe harbor provisions to facilitate compliance with anti-discrimination requirements. Rather than engaging in the annual process of determining whether or not they have met the regular discrimination tests, companies can be assured that their plan will be in compliance with these requirements if they adopt either of two "safe harbor" plan alternatives:

- **The 3% Employer Contribution.** This alternative requires the employer to make a contribution equal to at least 3% of compensation for each employee eligible to make deferrals regardless of whether or not they make 401(k) elective deferrals.

- **The Employer Match Safe Harbor.** This choice requires that the plan must provide a matching contribution of at least 4% of an employee's compensation. The match must be dollar-for-dollar on the employee's deferrals of up to 3% of compensation and fifty cents for each dollar on the next 2% of compensation deferred. Thus an employee must defer 5% of compensation to get the 4% employer match. Under this safe harbor alternative, an employee who does not defer any salary to the plan receives no employer match.

For either safe harbor option, employer contributions to the plan must be immediately 100% vested, and the company may not make the contribution conditional on year-end employment. Employers whose 401(k) plans do not use the safe harbor provisions or the anti-discrimination requirements often engage in the following activities for the purpose of increasing participation by lower-paid employees and thereby passing the tests:

- Provide a company matching contribution or increase the existing match (subject to Internal Revenue Code contribution limits).

- Allow employees to borrow from their 401(k) plans, thereby making these funds available for emergencies or major expenses such as home purchases or financing a child's college education.

- Provide rapid or immediate vesting for employer matching contributions to the plan.

Being Prudent with Employer Stock in a 401(k)

With each downturn in the business cycle, reports appear in the news media of businesses that have failed and left thousands of employees holding large amounts of the company's near-worthless stock in their 401(k) accounts. In 2001, it was Enron Corporation. Previous downturns featured, among others, ColorTile Corporation and Broadway-Hale Stores.

These reports generate understandable concern about the practice of holding significant quantities of employer stock in 401(k) retirement savings accounts. Company policies that require employees to hold the matching stock they receive, in effect barring them from cashing out that stock (at least until reaching a certain age) and reinvesting in other assets, have drawn the attention of regulators and legislators. A company contemplating the use of a 401(k) plan that will hold company stock should be aware of the issues and have a well thought out strategic response.

Observations and Lessons Learned

Some fundamental principles can be drawn from the experience of Enron and its predecessors that may suggest how a company can prudently and responsibly use a 401(k) plan as a vehicle for employee ownership:

1. Employee stock ownership and retirement saving are two separate and distinct goals. Certainly, each is valuable and there is a role for each. While it may be possible, to a limited degree, to pursue both goals at the same time through the same vehicle, neither employers nor employees should lose sight of the fact that the two goals are independent.

2. Today's 401(k) plans are in most cases "participant directed." This means that each employee makes the decisions (usually based on a limited menu of choices) as to how his account will be invested. Employees can make those decisions wisely, however, only if they have a solid understanding of investment principles and practices. Companies that establish participant directed 401(k) plans may have a moral, if not legal, obligation to provide a program of investment education that will equip employees to handle the investment responsibilities that go with such plans.

3. The principal of diversification in retirement savings is still valid. Most financial advisors continue to recommend that employees have at least a portion of their retirement savings invested in a prudently diversified fashion so as to minimize overall risk and maximize the likelihood that a reliable nest egg will be there when retirement comes. Only when adequate provision has been made for a well-diversified component of retirement savings should an employee feel free to invest more speculatively. That's when employer stock can begin to do double duty—as both employee ownership and retirement savings.

4. While retirement savings programs should seek to limit risk to the extent possible without unduly lowering investment returns, risk is not only acceptable but, within limits, desirable, in an employee ownership program. The cornerstone concept of employee ownership is, after all, that the employees will benefit according to the fortunes of the company. While assessments of employee ownership tend to focus on the upside potential of this proposition, it is clear that this is not a one-way street.

A corporate policy of making 401(k) matching contributions in the form of company stock—and requiring the recipients to continue to hold that stock up to a certain age—can be an effective and appropriate method of creating employee ownership. Companies that take this route, however, should also provide employees with the opportunity to secure some of their retirement savings in lower risk investment alternatives (such as a traditional "defined benefit" pension plan or well-diversified investment funds), and provide sufficient education on investment principles to assure that employees' decisions will be fully informed ones.

KSOPs

There are a number of situations where it is practical and advisable for a company to combine its current 401(k) with an ESOP. This is commonly referred to as a KSOP. Combining the plans allows the corporate match on the 401(k) to fund the debt payment obligations on a leveraged ESOP and/or to capture the tax deduction for dividends paid on ESOP stock. In addition, combining the plans reduces administrative expenses and facilitates transfer of assets between the plans as appropriate.

In a typical KSOP arrangement, the sponsoring company matches employee 401(k) contributions with a contribution of cash or corporate stock to the employee's ESOP account. If a cash contribution is made, it can be used to help repay the debt of a leveraged ESOP transaction (see Chapter Six on leveraged ESOPs). As with a stand-alone 401(k) plan, employee salary deferrals are invested in various diversified investment accounts.

Similarly, the 401(k) portion of the KSOP can provide a convenient means of transferring assets from the ESOP accounts of employees approaching retirement age who choose to exercise their ESOP diversification option. Employees who elect to diversify their ESOP accounts can simply direct that the cash equivalent of those ESOP shares be transferred to their 401(k) account.

Another advantage of KSOPs is that dividends paid on stock held by an ESOP are generally tax deductible for the corporation. If the plan were simply a 401(k) with a portion of the plan assets invested in employer securities, any dividends paid on the stock would not be deductible.

It should be noted that IRS regulations require that the ESOP and 401(k) portions of KSOPs be tested separately for purposes of determining whether the plan discriminates in favor of highly compensated employees. Because anti-discrimination rules are different for 401(k) plans and ESOPs, care must be taken to ensure that both the ESOP and the 401(k) anti-discrimination tests are met.

OTHER QUALIFIED BENEFIT PLANS

Qualified benefit plans such as deferred profit sharing plans and money purchase pension plans typically limit the amount of plan assets that are invested in company stock. Unlike ESOPs, which are required by law to be primarily invested in employer securities, assets of these plans are generally invested in a diversified portfolio. Profit sharing plans generally, and money purchase plans particularly, are not designed for significant investment in company stock, though company stock is acceptable as part of the asset mix of the plan. Because of the fiduciary standards for asset diversification and prohibited transaction rules, it is generally advisable that not more than 30% to 40% of profit sharing plan assets nor more than 10% of money purchase plan assets be invested in company stock, though some profit sharing plans (and some 401(k) plans) do have special provisions allowing the plan to include a higher percentage of company stock.

A defined benefit pension plan is designed to provide participants with a fixed monthly payment at retirement. The benefit is usually based on a formula that incorporates an employee's compensation and length of employment. Most companies fund such plans through a diversified portfolio of stocks and bonds which, by law, may not contain more than 10% of the plan's assets in company stock. Defined benefit plans rarely invest in company stock for fiduciary and other reasons, though the practice is more common among publicly traded companies. Because these plans are not individual account plans, employees never actually receive the company stock as a benefit, but the performance of the stock can contribute to the growth of the plan's assets.

TAX AND COST IMPLICATIONS

Qualified retirement plans offer tax incentives to both employers and employees. Subject to maximum contribution limits, company contributions of cash or stock to these plans are fully tax deductible. The 401(k) salary deferral allows employees to defer a portion of their compensation to a retirement trust, which reduces taxable income, while gains on the investment in the trust are tax-deferred until it is distributed.

Except for special "hardship" situations in 401(k) plans, distributions generally may not be made from qualified plans until the employee terminates employment or attains retirement age (59½ in many plans). However, most 401(k) plans generally permit participants to borrow against their 401(k) plan account (subject to a limit of 50% of their vested account balance, or $50,000, if less). If a distribution is made before the employee turns 59½ due to termination of employment (or hardship withdrawal, in a 401(k) plan) the employee is subject to ordinary income taxes, and a 10% federal penalty for early withdrawal may also apply. Some states also impose penalty taxes for early withdrawals. However, if the employee arranges a direct transfer of the distribution proceeds to another qualified retirement plan or individual retirement account (IRA), tax will continue to be deferred. All of the tax incentives afforded to ESOPs are applied to the ESOP portion of a KSOP (see ESOP Tax Implications in Chapter Six).

Qualified retirement plans are generally more expensive to establish and administer than direct stock purchase, stock grant or stock option plans. A basic 401(k) plan without a corporate equity component can usually be established for under $5,000.

Adding an equity component to the 401(k) plan can increase the cost by several thousand dollars. A non-leveraged KSOP can often cost anywhere from $15,000 to $20,000 to set up, while a leveraged KSOP can cost significantly more depending upon its complexity.

Ongoing costs associated with the management of a qualified plan can amount to several thousand dollars per year depending on its size, number of participants and complexity. In addition, compliance with the Internal Revenue Code and ERISA regulations requires an annual independent appraisal to establish the fair market value of company securities if they are not publicly traded. The fee for the initial valuation for a qualified plan is typically a minimum of $10,000 and can be substantially higher, depending on the size and complexity of the company. For subsequent annual valuations, it is normally less.

A plan with 100 or more participants also requires an annual audit by a certified public accountant. This can cost from $5,000 to $10,000 per year. Plans with fewer than 100 participants may require an audit in certain limited situations.

If a company is planning to have both a 401(k) and an ESOP, combining the plans to form a KSOP can meet all the objectives of both plans and may reduce administrative costs, as the audit, tax preparation, legal and communication requirements are combined in a single plan.

ADVANTAGES AND DRAWBACKS

Advantages

- All qualified retirement plans allow the company to take a current tax deduction for contributions to the plan while permitting the assets of the plan to accumulate tax-deferred until distributed to employees.
- 401(k) plans allow employees to save for retirement with pre-tax dollars.
- A company can fund its contribution with employer stock, reducing the immediate cash requirements needed to fund the plan and offering employees an opportunity to gain ownership in the company.
- Providing employer stock as an investment option allows employees to invest in employer stock on a pre-tax basis.
- Employee investments in employer stock can generate capital for the corporation.
- 401(k) plans can be established at a relatively low cost to the employer and offer both employers and employees a great deal of flexibility and discretion in terms of plan design and investment alternatives.

Drawbacks

- Offering employer stock as an investment alternative raises securities compliance and disclosure requirements and, in private companies, may make it difficult to find a trustee for the plan.
- 401(k) plans must meet IRS requirements for anti-discrimination. When combined with an ESOP in a KSOP arrangement, the 401(k)

and ESOP portions of the plan must be tested separately for anti-discrimination requirements.

- For private companies, using employer stock in a 401(k) plan requires hiring an independent appraiser to value the stock.

- Adding employer stock to a qualified retirement plan will generally increase the cost to establish and administer the plan.

- 401(k) plans holding employer stock have come under increased scrutiny. As a result, company sponsors should be sure to avoid plan design features that limit employees' ability to diversify their retirement plan assets.

- Qualified plans do not allow the company to arbitrarily pick and choose who may participate in the plan. Essentially all employees who meet Internal Revenue Code minimum participation standards must be allowed to participate. (There are some exceptions to this rule, but any exclusions from participation should be done only with the assistance of experts.)

- Sometimes qualified plans are regarded by employees as entitlement benefits and may not serve as incentive compensation.

ACCOUNTING CONSIDERATIONS

Generally, contributions made to a 401(k) plan (employee pre-tax or employer match) are reported as compensation and recorded on the company's financial statements in accordance with generally accepted accounting principles. Any changes in the value of the 401(k) assets are not recorded on the company's books. In addition, accounting records are not affected when distributions are made from the 401(k) plan. To the extent that an ESOP is incorporated into the 401(k), making it a KSOP, the accounting rules are the same as an ESOP. See Chapter Six for ESOP accounting considerations.

Chapter Eight

Non-Qualified Deferred Compensation Plans

N on-qualified deferred compensation plans are traditionally used to defer taxes and build wealth for key executives. In the past, these plans were quite flexible and were used to meet tax planning and compensation objectives for specific employees or groups of employees. When combined with the use of company stock, non-qualified plans are ideal for providing key executives with a long term incentive to help build shareholder value over the course of their career with the company. As a result of tax legislation passed in 2004, the design of deferred compensation programs has been restricted substantially, but these programs will likely still be a common feature in many executive compensation programs.

HOW THEY WORK

Deferred compensation arrangements fundamentally consist of an agreement between an employer and an employee that payments due for current services will be made at a future date. The employee's tax objective is to defer taxes on the compensation, including any increase in the value of the amount deferred, until the payments are actually received. For the company the result is, in part, a tax timing charge. The company forgoes current compensation deductibility and receives tax deductibility at the time of the payout. In addition, to the extent that the arrangement is unfunded and the company has the use of the deferred compensation during the deferral period, these arrangements can improve the company's profitability, if the return earned by the company on the after-tax deferred funds is greater than the interest or other return rate credited to the employee on the deferred funds.

With these plans, eligibility is restricted to a select group of management and highly compensated employees who wish to defer compensation. The employee typically elects to defer a portion of his future compensation (generally, salary and/or bonuses). The company establishes an account to track the amount deferred by the employee, or the company can simply make a promise to provide deferred payments at a future specified date.

There are various informal funding strategies that can be used to manage the employee's account. The value of the deferred compensation could change based on any of a variety of formulas such as a fixed interest rate, the fluctuation value of investment sub-accounts, the value of company stock or other similar investments. The plan could specify when the distribution would be made to the employee, generally at a specified date (for example, after three years), at termination of employment or upon retirement. When the distribution is made, the employee pays ordinary income taxes on the value of the distribution and the company qualifies for a corresponding tax deduction.

Because these plans are typically intended to benefit a select group of key executives, it is important that they be structured to qualify for exemptions from ERISA (so that the plan does not have to be provided to all employees) and to avoid having contributions to the plan and earnings on plan assets become subject to current taxation.

Deferred compensation plans are sometimes designed to supplement the benefits that key employees receive under qualified plans such as 401(k) plans, ESOPs or defined benefit pension plans. These are commonly called SERPs, or supplemental executive retirement plans.

Deferred compensation plans are also used for purposes other than retirement planning. For example, some employers require that a portion of executives' bonuses be deferred for a few years and be notionally invested in employer stock during that period. These programs are intended to promote retention of these executives during the vesting period as well as focus them on stock performance. Some purely voluntary programs permit employees to elect to defer compensation for a fixed time period (often three, five or 10 years) or until retirement. These programs are generally provided to improve the tax-effectiveness of the compensation received by the employee. In that regard, the higher the rate of personal tax, the greater the after-tax return will be as a result of deferring the compensation, as compared to investing the after-tax compensation directly.

The benefits of such a deferral strategy can be illustrated by the following example:

Deferred Compensation Example

Assumptions:

Pat elects to defer the receipt of a $10,000 bonus for 10 years.
The bonus is notionally invested in two investments, with the
indicated rates of return:

- Interest income   4% per year
- Employer stock   10% per year

Pat's current and expected retirement marginal tax rate is 34%

Tax rate applicable to capital gains is 15%

Account value at end of deferral period (pre-tax)	$20,370
Less tax:	$ (6,926)
After tax value at end of 10 years	$13,444
If Pat did not defer but invested the after-tax bonus ($6,600) 50/50 in the same investments: • Interest earned taxed as ordinary income each year and after-tax amount reinvested • Employer stock held throughout period and disposed of at end of 10 years	
After-tax value at end of 10 years	$12,053
Increase in after-tax holdings as result of deferral	$ 1,391

SECTION 409A

Section 409A governing the tax treatment of nonqualified deferred compensation plans was added to the Internal Revenue Code effective January 1, 2005. Section 409A prescribes the timing of initial and subsequent deferral arrangements, specifies when and how distribution elections may be made and changed, restricts distribution events, prohibits the acceleration of payments, and imposes certain funding restrictions on deferred compensation arrangements.

In the past, it was common to permit participants in voluntary deferred compensation plans to elect to further delay the receipt of the deferred amounts, so long as the election was made prior to the actual receipt of the deferred amounts. Section 409A now imposes significant restrictions to such subsequent elective deferrals.

Deferral Elections

In order to avoid current taxation, the employee must elect to defer the compensation before it is actually earned. Different timing rules for initial deferral elections apply to "performance-based" and "non-performance based" deferred compensation.

- For non-performance-based compensation paid to individuals (such as salary), the deferral election must be made before the end of the prior calendar year, except in the first year of plan eligibility, in which case the election must be made within 30 days of first becoming eligible to participate in the program.
- For performance based compensation (such as bonuses where the amount payable is based on services performed over a period of at least 12 months), the election to defer compensation must be made no later than 6 months before the end of the period.[13]

In addition, for subsequent deferrals (those made after the award is initially granted and where an initial deferral election has been made), the requirements for making a deferral election to further delay the receipt of the compensation are quite daunting. These deferral elections must be made at least 12 months prior to any amount being payable and the elected deferral period must generally be at least an additional five years from when the amount would otherwise have been paid.

REQUIREMENTS FOR NON-TAXABILITY

Assuming that the proper deferral elections have been made, in order to avoid deferred compensation plan status, deferred amounts must then be either:

- subject to a substantial risk of forfeiture (see below) during the deferral period or
- payable at a defined fixed time or on a fixed schedule, subject to acceleration (or delay) only if certain strict guidelines are met.

The downside of falling afoul of these deferred compensation plan tax rules is substantial—an employee could be immediately subject to taxability on the deferred amount, and would be required to pay a penalty equal to 20% of the deferred amount plus interest.

Substantial Risk of Forfeiture. Under the prior law, being a general creditor of the employer was sufficient to create a substantial risk of forfeiture. However, a substantial risk of forfeiture is now established only where the entitlement to payment is conditioned on the performance of:

---

13 Note that performance-based compensation does not include amounts based on appreciation in employer stock or arrangements where the performance criteria are substantially certain to be met at the time they are set.

- substantial future services by any person (usually the employee)[14] or
- the occurrence of a condition related to a purpose of the compensation (such as a required level of earnings, or a liquidity event), and the possibility of forfeiture is substantial.

As a result, generally only rights that are "unvested" in the usual sense of the term (that there are substantive service or performance-related conditions that must be met prior to the compensation vesting) will be considered to be subject to a substantial risk of forfeiture.

Most voluntary deferred compensation programs would not be subject to a substantial risk of forfeiture, since the employee's entitlement to the amounts is absolute. However, many other types of deferred compensation programs (particularly deferred bonus programs that are conditioned on continued service or attaining particular performance standards) would be subject to a substantial risk of forfeiture until such point as the condition was satisfied.

Fixed Payment Schedule. In the alternative, deferred amounts that are not subject to a substantial risk of forfeiture will not be currently taxable if they are required to be paid under a fixed schedule. Under the new Section 409A deferred compensation plan rules, employees will be able to defer tax on accrued amounts if entitlements under the program cannot be distributed until a specified time or under a fixed schedule. Payments can only be made prior to the fixed distribution schedule in the following events and only if the plan permits earlier distribution in those circumstances:

- termination of employment (in which case certain senior executives are subject to an additional 6 month waiting period).
- disability.
- death.
- corporate change of control.
- an unforeseeable emergency.
- a requirement to pay related FICA taxes (and related income taxes) or to comply with a domestic relations order or conflict-of-interest legislation.

No Economic Benefit or Constructive Receipt. Finally, there can be no "economic benefit" to the employee under the program. A compensation arrangement that provides a current economic benefit to an executive can result in current taxation to the executive even if he has no current right to receive cash

---

14 An agreement to not compete with the employer post-termination does not qualify as substantial future services.

or property. In order to avoid economic benefit, the promise to pay benefits under the plan must be unfunded[15] and unsecured. In addition, the employee could not be considered to have "constructively received" the deferred amount.

SPECIAL 409A REQUIREMENTS FOR EQUITY-BASED ARRANGEMENTS

The following equity-based deferred compensation arrangements are exempt from Section 409A requirements:

- Incentive stock options (ISOs).
- Section 423 employee stock purchase plans (ESPPs).
- Non-qualified stock options (NSOs) if the exercise price of the option can never be less than the fair market value of the underlying stock on the grant date, and there are no deferral features that would delay the recognition of income beyond the exercise date.
- Stock appreciation rights (SARs) if the base price can never be less than the fair market value of the underlying stock on the grant date and there are no other deferral features other than deferral of income to exercise the SAR.

To qualify for the exemptions from Section 409A, equity-based plans must be based on common stock that is not subject to any preferences as to dividends or liquidation rights.[16] Common stock of a parent corporation can qualify with respect to awards to individuals who perform services for a subsidiary, provided the parent owns stock representing at least 50% of the fair market value or voting power of the subsidiary.

Section 409A also establishes requirements for determining the fair market value (FMV) of the stock used in deferred compensation plans, as follows:

For stock readily tradable on an established securities market:

- The last sale price before, or the first sale price after, the grant; the closing selling price on the grant date or the immediately preceding trading day; or any other reasonable basis using actual transactions.
- It is also permissible to use an average selling price over a specified period of 30 days before or 30 days after the grant if the terms of the offer are specified before the start of the averaging period and such method is used consistently for all grants under the program.

For stock not readily tradable on an established securities market:

---

15 To be considered unfunded, plan assets must remain unsecured and the participant may not have access to the assets or transfer the assets to another beneficiary.
16 American Depository Receipts (ADRs) qualify under this definition of common stock.

- A value determined by the reasonable application of a reasonable valuation method. Factors which must be taken into account to meet the reasonableness test should include the value of the tangible and intangible assets of the corporation, the present value of future cash flows, the market value of stock or equity interests in similar corporations or entities engaged in substantially the same business, and other relevant factors such as control premiums or minority discounts. All available information material to the corporation must be considered.

- Valuations established by an independent appraiser within 12 months of the grant date, or a consistently applied valuation formula based on the tax principles governing the valuation of shares subject to non-lapse restrictions, will be presumed to meet the standard of reasonableness.

- For a start-up company that is less than 10 years old, a written valuation report taking into account the valuation factors referenced above and prepared by a person with significant knowledge and experience or training in performing similar valuations is also permissible.

ERISA ISSUES

For all non-qualified deferred compensation plans, it is important that the plan qualify as a "top-hat" plan for IRS and ERISA purposes. In order to qualify, a plan must be both unfunded and must benefit only a select group of management or highly compensated employees. It is vital that the employees included in a top-hat plan be limited not only in number but also in rank, so that the plan will be select. Top-hat plans are exempt from the participation, vesting, funding and fiduciary requirements of ERISA, but are subject to limited reporting and disclosure requirements. The most significant of these reporting requirements is that the employer must file a brief, one-time disclosure statement within 120 days of plan inception and be prepared to provide plan documents upon request.

FUNDING THROUGH A RABBI TRUST

A common concern about deferred compensation plans (particularly those that will pay distributions on or after retirement) is that the employer may either refuse to pay ("change of heart") or be unable to pay the deferred amounts when due. While it is not possible to give participants full security that their benefits will be paid even in the event of insolvency (since this would no longer constitute a substantial risk of forfeiture), it is possible to provide assurances that the employer

---

Key Points for Non-Qualified Deferred Compensation Arrangements

- Non-qualified deferred compensation can be tailored with some flexibility to fit precise objectives for specific employees or groups of employees.
- They allow executives to voluntarily defer receipt (and therefore current taxation) of a portion of salary and/or bonus.
- To preserve the tax deferral, the election to defer compensation must be made before prescribed times, depending upon the type of compensation, and must be paid according to fixed timetables.
- Income on deferred monies can be based on fixed or variable interest rates, a published financial index (such as prime rate or stock market index), performance of employer stock or other financial criteria determined by the company.
- Payout typically occurs upon termination of employment or retirement, or according to a fixed date or schedule. Upon distribution, the employee recognizes ordinary income in the year of payout and the company takes a corresponding tax deduction.
- Plans must qualify as "unfunded," but funding assets may be set aside in a Rabbi Trust that would be subject to the claims of general creditors in the event of company insolvency or bankruptcy.

---

will not have a "change of heart" through the use of a Rabbi Trust.[17] A Rabbi Trust is an irrevocable trust in which assets are set aside for the exclusive use of satisfying an employer's contractual obligation to pay deferred compensation. It can be funded in any manner including cash, insurance or company stock. Rabbi Trust assets are subject to the claims of general creditors but are inaccessible to the company for discretionary use until benefit obligations are met.

The Rabbi Trust has become quite common in deferred compensation planning. Early Treasury Department regulations in the income tax area provided that a transfer was taxable when assets were set aside in trust or escrow "beyond the reach of the employer's creditors." This suggests that assets which are set aside, but not beyond the reach of the employer's creditors, would not be taxable.

---

17 A Rabbi Trust is technically a "grantor trust," but received its name because the earliest IRS approval of such an arrangement was for a deferred compensation program provided by a congregation to its rabbi.

Using Equity in Deferred Compensation Arrangements

- Employer grants stock to employee or employee defers salary to purchase stock.
- Stock is contributed to a Rabbi Trust.
- Employee's deferred account grows with the value of the stock.
- Distributions can be made in cash or stock.
- Employee is exempt from income taxes until a distribution is received from the trust, at which time he is taxed at ordinary income rates and the corporation qualifies for a corresponding tax deduction.
- For accounting purposes, the employer records an expense on the income statement based on the value of the stock transferred to the trust. This expense is spread over the vesting period, if any.
- For tax and accounting purposes growth, gains or dividends on employer stock held by the Rabbi Trust will be disregarded at the corporate level. However, any gains or income earned by the Rabbi Trust on other types of plan assets will be attributed to the corporate employer for both accounting and tax purposes.
- The Rabbi Trust may include other cash-based deferred compensation awards to provide employees with sufficient liquidity to exercise stock options and/or pay taxes on stock distributions from the trust.

This concept was established by a long series of private letter rulings by the IRS, followed in 1992 by the publication of a model Rabbi Trust intended to be used as a safe harbor. In practice, the model trust has become more of a requirement than a safe harbor because the IRS announced that it would not issue rulings on any unfunded deferred compensation arrangements that use a trust other than the model trust, except in rare and unusual circumstances. In addition, the Department of Labor has ruled on several occasions that a top-hat plan supported by a Rabbi Trust is unfunded for purposes of Title I of ERISA, which ensures that the plan would not be subject to ERISA.

To incorporate employee ownership within a deferred compensation arrangement, the Rabbi Trust can be funded with employer stock. When a distribution is made from the Rabbi Trust, the employee can receive the distribution either in stock or in cash equal to the fair market value of the stock. It is important that the employees do not have rights to particular shares of stock—instead the assets in the trust are to be used at the discretion of the trustee/employer to pay the promised benefits.

TAX AND COST IMPLICATIONS

If properly structured, a deferred compensation plan allows an employee to defer taxes on future compensation. Even though the employer will have incurred an accounting expense for the deferred compensation, no tax deduction can be claimed until the deferred compensation is actually paid or otherwise included in the income of the recipient, so the employer's corporate income taxes will be higher than they would have been had the amount not been deferred. At distribution, the employee would pay ordinary income tax on the value of the distribution and the company would qualify for a corresponding tax deduction.

The cost of implementing a non-qualified deferred compensation plan may be as low as $5,000, depending upon plan complexity. These plans can be administered in house, but more often are administered by the provider of the initial plan design or by the provider of any informal funding arrangement. If a Rabbi Trust is used, there are additional costs associated with establishing the trust.

ADVANTAGES AND DRAWBACKS

Advantages

- Non-qualified deferred compensation plans are fairly flexible and can be designed to suit any number of specific individual and corporate compensation objectives.
- "Non-discrimination" restrictions do not apply to non-qualified plans; employers have great latitude in creating plans for key employees.
- Compensation in excess of the maximum permitted for qualified plans can be deferred in non-qualified plans.
- Accumulated investment value, defined as the initial deferral and any earnings, is not subject to taxation until the compensation is paid.

Guidelines for Preserving Tax Deferral

Following these guidelines will help ensure that a plan will be recognized by the IRS as unfunded in order to take advantage of the favorable tax treatment:

- The deferred amount must be subject to the claims of general creditors.
- The promise to pay the deferred amount must be a mere contractual obligation of the employer, not evidenced by notes or secured in any way.
- The election to defer must be made before the beginning of the period of service for which the compensation is payable.
- The deferred amount must be payable at a specific date or time, subject to acceleration only in limited defined circumstances, unless the plan imposes a substantial forfeiture provision that remains in effect throughout the entire deferral period.
- The plan must define the time and method whereby the employee will receive a distribution. The plan must state clearly that participants have the status of general unsecured creditors of the company.
- The plan must specifically prohibit the transfer or alienation of a participant's interest.
- The plan must state that it is the intention of the parties that the arrangement be unfunded for tax purposes and for purposes of Title I of ERISA.
- If the plan uses a trust, the trust must take the form of the model Rabbi Trust described in IRS Revenue Procedure 92-64 except in rare and unusual circumstances. Employers should always request a letter ruling from the IRS regarding any proposed trust not based on the model Rabbi Trust.

Drawbacks

- Plans must be limited to a select group of employees and therefore are not suitable for broad-based equity sharing.
- Plan assets are subject to the claims of the employer's creditors in the event of company insolvency or bankruptcy. An employee has no rights to the assets other than as a general unsecured creditor.

- Vested contributions to deferred compensation accounts must be charged as a current expense on the company's books. Unvested contributions and related earnings are reflected as an expense over the vesting period. Any growth or earnings on plan assets (other than company stock) held in a Rabbi Trust will need to be expensed on the company's financial statement.
- The company forgoes a tax deduction for deferred amounts (even if vested) during the deferral period.
- There are severe tax penalties for violation of the deferred compensation rules under Internal Revenue Code Section 409A.
- Rabbi Trusts must be established based on a model set forth by the IRS or by obtaining a private letter ruling. Rabbi Trusts are not operative under the laws of some states.

ACCOUNTING CONSIDERATIONS

Deferred compensation must be expensed on the company's books as it vests. As the account is credited with earnings (except when company stock is held by a Rabbi Trust), an additional expense is recorded. This can result in significant additional current compensation expense. If the plan is a voluntary deferral plan, the incremental expense to the company is only that of the earnings portion of the account balance, since the salary and/or bonus was an expense which was already booked. To account for the earnings on the account balance, the company would record a deferred tax asset and would book a corresponding liability based on the value of the account.

When company stock is issued to a Rabbi Trust, the company is required to book an expense and a liability based on the value of the stock at the time of grant. Additional increases in the value of the stock or dividends would not be booked as an expense.

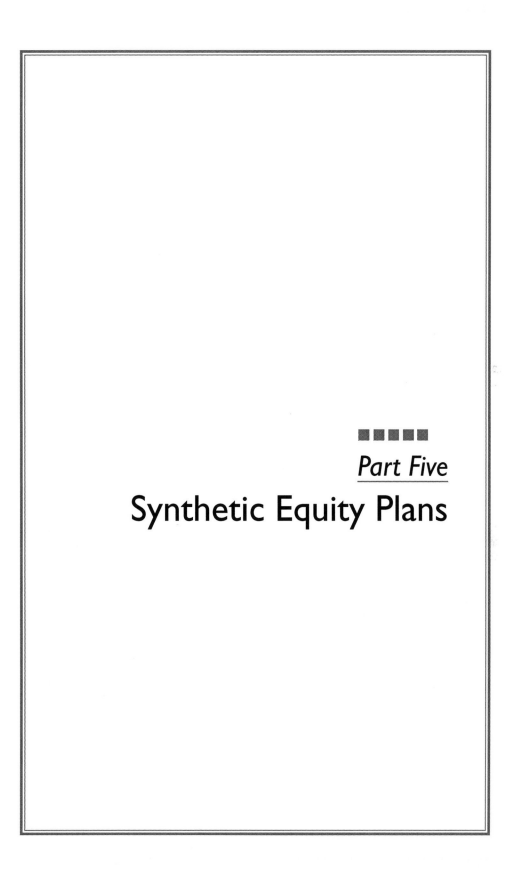

Part Five

Synthetic Equity Plans

Chapter Nine

Stock Appreciation Rights and Phantom Stock

Synthetic equity refers to any of several types of specialized deferred compensation techniques designed to provide employees with the economic benefits of stock ownership without actually transferring stock.

Synthetic equity awards are intended to simulate the value of a predetermined number of shares of stock of the sponsoring company over a specific period of time. Synthetic equity is commonly used in situations where companies are unable or unwilling to alter their existing ownership structure, but nevertheless wish to provide employees with incentive compensation based on the actual performance of the business. In some cases, an award of synthetic equity can be made subject to the performance of divisions or subsidiary organizations, though its actual value is usually based on the stock of the sponsoring corporation. Two of the most common forms of synthetic equity are stock appreciation rights (SARs) and phantom stock.

HOW THEY WORK

Stock Appreciation Rights

SARs are an unsecured promise by the company to pay an employee compensation based on the appreciation in the value of a specified number of underlying common shares of the company. They are conceptually similar to stock options in that the exercise of the SAR entitles the employee only to the appreciation in value, not the underlying value of the stock at the time of grant. In contrast to options, which require the employee to purchase the underlying stock at the grant price upon exercising the option, SARs require no cash outlay from the employee who simply receives the net appreciated value of the SAR at exercise. The SAR awards themselves are typically paid in cash.

The design of synthetic equity awards was altered dramatically by Section 409A of the Internal Revenue Code enacted in late 2004 which regulates deferred compensation arrangements. (See Chapter Eight for a detailed discussion of Section 409A requirements). SARs, however, can be exempt from the 409A requirements if the base price of the SAR can never be less than the fair market value of the underlying common stock on the grant date, and there are no deferral features other than deferral of income to exercise the SAR. SARs are also subject to the valuation guidelines for deferred compensation plans governed by Section 409A.

SARs are generally effective for a fixed number of years from the grant date. They are typically subject to vesting conditions such that any unvested portion of the SAR is forfeited if the employee terminates employment prior to the designated vesting dates. The most common method for granting SARs is to base them on the market value of the sponsoring corporation's actual stock, though SARs can be valued based on the computed or actual value of a division or subsidiary of the parent company. In some cases, the vesting of the SAR award may be accelerated when the company, or any division or subsidiary, achieves other performance targets such as earnings, book value, percentage of profits, percentage of operating cash flow above a return threshold, or percentage of economic value added (a measure of economic returns above the cost of capital).

Phantom Stock

Phantom stock represents units of value that correspond to an equivalent number of shares of stock granted to an employee for a specific period of time. They are conceptually similar to a restricted stock grant. Upon maturity/vesting, the employee is compensated in cash, based on the value of the phantom stock. Unlike SARs, the amount of compensation on phantom shares may include the underlying value of the unit itself as well as any appreciation above the grant price. Phantom stock plans can include the right to receive compensation equal to any dividends paid on the underlying stock ("dividend equivalents") during the period in which the phantom shares are held. Such dividends can either be paid currently or notionally reinvested in further phantom stock when the phantom shares mature.

Payments from phantom shares have typically been based on a fixed payout schedule, so the fact that they are subject to the new Section 409A deferred compensation plan rules[18] has not significantly affected their design. If the vesting of the phantom stock is tied to the satisfaction of performance factors that qualify

---

18 This includes requirements relating to the valuation of the underlying shares.

as performance-based compensation under Section 409A, then the initial deferral election may be made at any time prior to the last six months of the performance vesting period.

TAX AND COST IMPLICATIONS

If structured properly, there are generally no tax consequences to the company or the employee upon grant of a SAR or phantom stock unit. Tax is generally deferred until the exercise of the SAR or the payment of the phantom share unit. In the past, it was not uncommon to have SARs that were granted in tandem with stock options. These arrangements occasionally took the form of an either/or grant—if the employee exercised the SAR, the corresponding option would be forfeited and vice versa. Alternatively, some employers granted tandem SARs to generate a source of cash for employees to use to pay their withholding tax liability occasioned by the exercise of the related option. Neither of these arrangements is acceptable under the new Section 409A rules, making such an approach problematic.

Neither SARs nor phantom stock receive any preferential tax treatment, nor is any deferral of the tax permitted beyond the time of payment. SARs and phantom stock both represent a future cash liability to the company equivalent to the appreciation value of SARs or phantom shares, respectively.

INNOVATIVE APPROACHES

SARs and phantom stock can facilitate the flexible design of long-term incentive programs. The vesting of the awards, for example, can be tied to targeted performance goals such as increases in sales, increases in return on investment or the performance of a particular subsidiary or division.

Another common strategy is to link voluntary deferred compensation plans with phantom stock. Executives who defer salaries or bonuses under an unfunded deferred compensation plan may notionally invest such deferred bonuses in phantom stock.

Similarly, phantom shares can be used to provide a performance-based retirement program for key employees. In such a plan, corporate contributions to the key employee retirement plan are subject to financial performance and then invested in phantom shares, with the ultimate value of the deferred funds tied to phantom share value.

Again, it is important that any of these voluntary deferred or retirement compensation programs meet the requirements of non-taxability as described in Chapter Eight.

Phantom stock or SARs are increasingly used by U.S. multi-national companies to provide the economic equivalent of options or restricted stock grants to employees of foreign subsidiaries or branches where local tax, securities or exchange control rules make the use of stock or stock options unfeasible.

SYNTHETIC EQUITY IN S CORPORATIONS

Because S Corporations are subject to a limit of 75 shareholders, synthetic equity can be a useful means of providing ownership incentives to a broad base of employees without jeopardizing the company's S Corporation status. Holders of SARs or phantom stock units are not generally counted against the 75-shareholder limit and are not subject to taxation as S Corporation shareholders.

Special considerations apply, however, when synthetic equity is used in S Corporations that include an ESOP. Because ESOPs in S Corporations are exempt from federal income taxes, many companies choose to structure their ownership so that the ESOP owns all or a significant majority of the company's stock. SARs are then provided to key employees as incentive compensation. Companies using synthetic equity in connection with an ESOP in an S Corporation must be aware that Section 409(p) rules relating to ESOPs in S Corporations specify that any form of synthetic equity is considered "deemed ownership" and subject to various tests to ensure that synthetic equity holders do not receive excessive economic benefits at the expense of the ESOP. Violation of the "deemed ownership" limits could subject the company to severe penalties. (See Chapter Six for a detailed discussion of S Corporation ESOPs.)

ADVANTAGES AND DRAWBACKS

Advantages
- Synthetic equity plans offer a means of providing employees with the long-term motivational benefits of stock appreciation and tie employee rewards to shareholder gains without diluting the owner-ship of existing shareholders.
- Synthetic equity avoids issues of minority shareholder rights where that is a concern.
- Vesting and deferred exercise rights coupled with multiple awards over time can serve as a performance-based retention tool similar to actual stock awards.
- Both SARs and phantom stock plans are adaptable to a variety of objectives.
- Synthetic equity plans are typically structured so that employees do

not have to actually purchase shares or exercise stock options, both of which require a cash outlay.

- For companies that are not publicly traded, establishing valuation formulas (subject to the guidelines of Internal Revenue Code Section 409A) for SARs and phantom stock can avoid the complexity and expense of hiring an independent valuation firm such as is required for ESOPs.
- Plans can be structured to reward the performance of divisions or subsidiaries.
- Companies can use synthetic equity to provide equity incentives to a broad base of employees without violating shareholder limits or restrictions.
- Not having to actually issue shares of stock avoids administrative and regulatory complexities that may occur with other types of plans.
- Synthetic equity can be a useful means of providing stock-like incentives to foreign employees. This is particularly true where the foreign jurisdiction does not tax SARs until exercise (in other words, they are taxable only on exercise, irrespective of earlier vesting). This can apply to foreign corporations or their U.S. subsidiaries for which issuing stock to U.S. employees may be impossible or impractical. It is also practical where local tax or regulatory limitations prevent the use of actual stock awards by foreign companies with employees in those jurisdictions.

Drawbacks

- For accounting purposes, SARs are considered liabilities and as such must be valued every year until they are completely settled.
- Synthetic equity plans represent a potentially significant cash drain on the company when an employee's cash entitlement matures.
- Whereas the exercise of an option may actually result in money coming into the company, the exercise of a SAR almost always creates a cash obligation for the company.
- There is no opportunity for capital gains treatment for SARs or phantom stock. Moreover, once SARs or phantom stock are paid out, the employee will have no further "ownership interest" in the company.

ACCOUNTING CONSIDERATIONS

- For accounting purposes, SARs are considered liabilities instead of equity and as such must be valued every year until they are completely settled. Subsequent variation in the value of the stock will typically result in ongoing adjustments to earnings.

• The value of a SAR for accounting purposes is determined by the application of an option pricing model, in the same manner that stock options, if granted, would be valued. See Chapter Four for more information on options pricing.

• Private companies have a choice in how they will reflect SARs for accounting purposes. They can either utilize the same method as public companies (outlined above, except that stock price volatility will generally be determined by reference to a peer group of public companies or a published industry index), or reflect the vested intrinsic value of the SARs as a compensation expense in each year. This methodology is much simpler for private companies, but may generate more unpredictable swings in compensation expense.

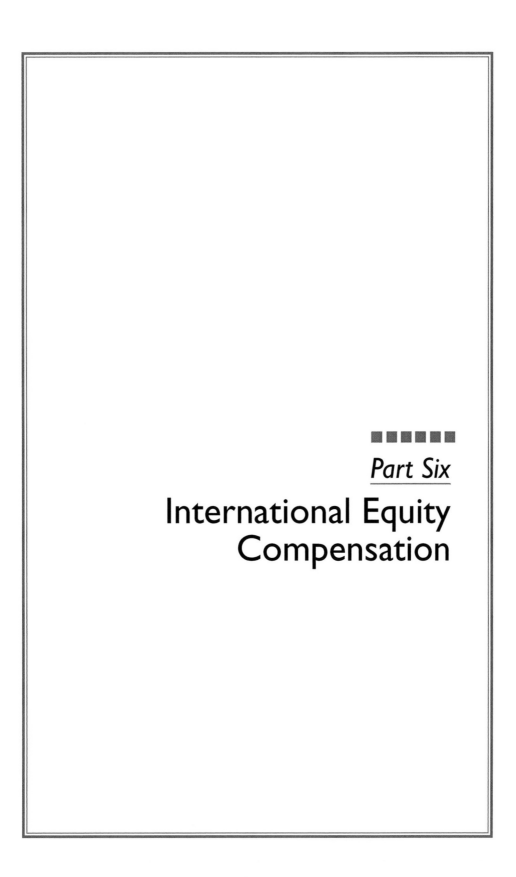

■ ■ ■ ■ ■ ■

Part Six

International Equity Compensation

Chapter Ten

Stock Programs for U.S. Companies Operating Abroad

The success of employee ownership in the United States has fueled growing interest in the use of broad-based equity compensation plans around the world. Dozens of countries have established laws and regulations governing the operation of employee stock plans. Some of these laws were created specifically for the purpose of defining the use of employee ownership within the context of the privatization of state-owned enterprises. Increasingly, however, other countries have approved laws facilitating the general operation of employee stock plans, including plans established by multi-national companies.

Many countries have adopted tax and regulatory policies governing the use of stock options or other stock-based programs as a direct result of the growth of stock plans among multi-national employers. This requires companies wanting to use stock to compensate and reward international employees to be familiar with and adhere to the laws in each country.

American companies operating abroad are sharing stock ownership with employees in increasing numbers. These companies have many reasons for doing so:

- To replicate the success of their U.S.-based plans in motivating employees to think and act like owners.
- To provide a common incentive and equitable treatment of their U.S. and non-U.S. employees.
- To help establish a common international identity for the corporation among its widespread workforce.
- To keep more of its stock in friendly hands.

- To provide continuity in benefits for expatriate employees on assignment in a foreign country.
- To provide international employees with U.S.-denominated securities, often an attractive benefit, especially in developing economies.

TYPES OF INTERNATIONAL PLANS

Stock Options

International equity plans can take several forms. The most common approach is to issue stock options. The granting methodology usually parallels the U.S. program for U.S. resident employees. However, it is sometimes important to adjust the size of grants (initial or ongoing) to take into account local compensation practices. For example, it is not uncommon that a typical U.S.-style grant would be worth several times the annual cash compensation of an employee in a third world country. In addition, in some less-developed countries, the concept of stock ownership is not well understood, so special efforts would have to be made to educate employees on the nature of the awards.

Some corporations make a one-time grant of a set number of options to each employee or grant equal numbers of options on an annual basis. Others provide employees with options equal in value to a given percentage of pay each year or provide option awards for selected employees based on individual merit.

One advantage of stock options is that they can usually be structured to avoid actual distribution of the shares, an approach that may be required in countries that restrict the ownership of stock in foreign companies. In a public company environment, this can be done through a cashless exercise of the options. A company or broker can provide international employees with a 24-hour loan facility whereby they can direct a designated broker in the United States to provide a loan sufficient to exercise their options. The broker then immediately sells all the shares, pays off the loan and transaction fees, and deposits the net proceeds into the employee's account. In this scenario, the employee does not actually take possession of the stock. This may seem contrary to the longer term goals of employee ownership, such as building a common identity or creating employee motivation, but in reality employees may still be driven to 'think like an owner' as long as they are holding options that can gain in value. And since the ultimate payment to the employee is in cash, this method avoids tax and securities compliance complexities.

International ESOP

Another approach to international equity plans is to create an "International ESOP" in a tax-free jurisdiction. Each of the company's international subsidiaries is provided with an account within the trust and each participating employee has an individual account within the plan of the appropriate subsidiary. Then, based on their individual profitability, the subsidiary corporations either purchase shares of the parent corporation or receive grants of stock from the parent, allocating those shares to the accounts of the participating employees by a pre-determined formula, usually a percent of salary.

The intent of this structure is to ensure that the shares are held in trust for the employees in the ESOP. At termination of service, the ESOP trustee sells the employee's shares and makes a distribution of the cash proceeds to the employee. As with the cashless option exercise referenced above, this has the advantage of alleviating securities registration concerns in most countries as well as avoiding certain country regulations restricting the ownership of shares in foreign corporations. Depending on local tax rules, the employee is simply taxed on amounts deposited to his account or the cash proceeds in accordance with the tax laws of the country where he resides. The shares are then reallocated to other employees within the ESOP trust.

Stock Purchase Plans, Restricted Stock Grants and Synthetic Equity

Some multi-national companies have successfully implemented stock purchase plans similar to Section 423 plans, though, as with stock options, the plan rules may need to be modified to conform to local laws. In these plans, the plan custodian typically collects after-tax employee salary contributions and makes periodic purchases of the stock on behalf of the employees. Tax-deferred programs similar to 401(k) plans that permit employees to invest their pre-tax contributions in company stock are available in some countries. Local laws will generally require the establishment of a separate plan for local employees.

Another common approach to avoiding securities law complexities or other prohibitions against holding stock in foreign countries is to provide restricted stock grants to key executives at overseas locations. The shares are held in trust on behalf of the employee until the restrictions lapse, at which time the employee can either receive the shares or request that the trustee sell the shares and distribute the sale proceeds to the employee. Whether a trust arrangement would be effective to protect the employee and the employer will depend on local law.

Offering synthetic equity incentives is another common strategy for avoiding securities registration complexities or providing equity incentives for employees in countries lacking formal securities laws. Similar in concept to stock appreciation rights or phantom shares, these plans are essentially deferred compensation agreements that provide cash payments based on the value of the underlying stock of the corporate sponsor. These plans are typically structured to mimic the benefits provided to other international employees but don't actually use company stock.

AREAS OF CONCERN

In establishing international equity plans, corporations need to recognize potential hurdles that can affect their strategy for equity participation:

- Registration requirements.
- Ownership and currency prohibitions and local employment law requirements.
- Unfavorable tax treatment.
- Currency rate volatility.

Registration Requirements

Separate securities laws apply in each country where employees will participate in the plan. In some cases, securities registration is required. Sometimes the registration process can be onerous, but often it is not as expensive or time-consuming as in the U.S. A number of countries provide exemption from local securities registration if the shares are already registered in the U.S., if the distribution is made only to employees, or if the employer has a limited number of shareholders in the country.

Ownership Prohibitions and Requirements

In some cases, currency exchange controls and employment laws are an important consideration in determining how employees will acquire their shares. For example, some countries prevent employees from owning foreign securities. Sometimes this prohibition can be overcome by using a cashless transaction. In some countries, it may be necessary to implement synthetic equity plans when securities restrictions prevent the use of foreign securities.

Some other jurisdictions prohibit or strictly limit local residents from holding foreign currency. In some cases, the plan may be established by making a special application to the country's central bank. In others, off-shore accounts are sometimes maintained for local residents, although the efficacy of these arrangements in insulating employees from their local restrictions is sometimes unclear.

In other jurisdictions, a corporate grant of stock as a benefit may be considered "regular and recurring," which means that such a grant is deemed to be part of an employees' standard compensation and may not be taken away from the employee, or may be subject to special severance or other retirement benefit calculations. In this case, it is important to clearly establish that a stock award is a one-time event based on current profitability or some other unique criteria. Another possible hurdle may exist in collective bargaining rules or other local labor laws.

Tax Treatment

It is important to note that rules governing the taxation of securities and stock options vary from country to country. These rules are often unclear in their application to U.S. plans and may be unfavorable from a tax perspective, although in some circumstances, the tax consequences of the arrangement may be more favorable than for U.S. participants. For example, it is sometimes difficult to ensure corporate deductibility of option gains or awards in the local jurisdiction. As more countries have introduced new rules or updated pre-existing stock option legislation, it has become increasingly important to ensure that multi-national plans are tailored to conform with the laws of each country in which employees receive options or other equity-based awards. Specific plan features, structure of legal entities, types of shares used and specific tax rulings obtained may affect particular legal and tax results.

Currency Volatility

Another factor contributing to the complexity of international stock plans is the issue of currency volatility. An American company's equity-based compensation program would normally be denominated in U.S. dollars, the value of which may vary considerably in terms of the local currency over a period of years during which the awards vest and/or reach their term.

Due to the complexities of international equity plans, the costs for such plans, including securities registration (if applicable), employee communications (often in multiple languages), custodial and legal fees, and plan administration can be substantially higher than comparable plans for domestic employees. The sponsoring company must be prepared to deal with tax, accounting and securities issues on a country-by-country basis, no matter which type of plan it may choose.

Nevertheless, the benefits of a common incentive, motivation and shared identity among multi-national employees in an increasingly global economy can be an attractive reason for establishing an international equity plan. Growing numbers of companies—including many small and medium-sized businesses which are operating in several different countries—are using stock incentives as a key strategy to motivate and reward their international employees.

Key Points for International Plans

When considering the establishment of an international equity plan, companies need to examine a number of important issues:

Securities and Currency Laws—Securities registration is sometimes required. Some countries' laws prohibit the ownership of shares in foreign corporations. An alternative approach in these jurisdictions may be to provide employees with phantom shares or stock appreciation rights, or to provide for cashless exercise of stock options so that the employee never acquires legal ownership of the shares.

Plan Administration—Careful coordination with the stock plan administrators in each foreign subsidiary is necessary in order to process employee purchases and make allocations to the appropriate accounts. Currency conversion issues are frequently a key administrative concern.

Taxation—Differing tax laws can make administration of a centrally managed plan difficult and require careful monitoring of changing tax law requirements.

Communications—Language and cultural barriers and local compensation practices should be given careful consideration in order to minimize difficulties.

Cost—The cost of international stock plans will vary considerably depending on how many and which countries are involved. Legal review of securities laws, tax complexities, plan administration and communications costs generally mean that these plans cost significantly more than domestic equivalents.

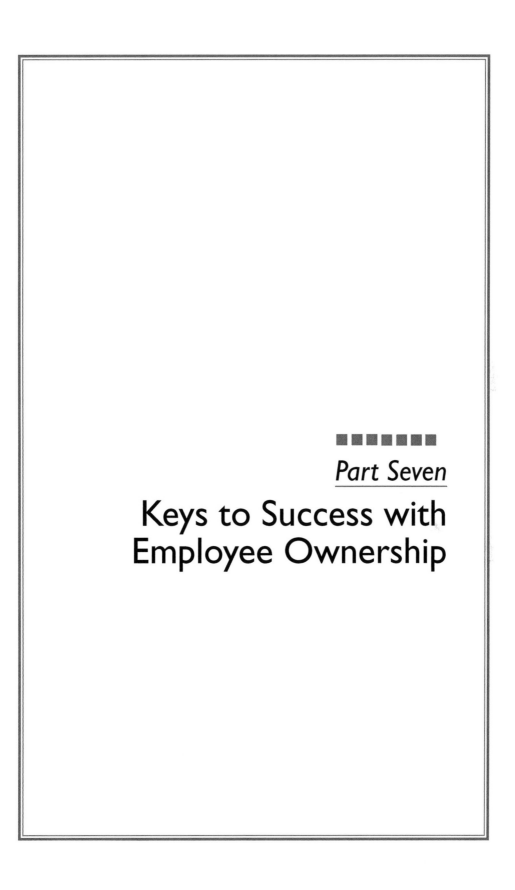

Part Seven

Keys to Success with Employee Ownership

Chapter Eleven

Critical Issues

There are a variety of critical issues associated with plan design and operational dynamics for equity compensation plans. The following questions highlight a number of issues that need to be considered in terms of managing an effective equity program. How these issues are addressed can provide a thoughtful rationale for the design of an equity-sharing program.

- Which employees will receive equity?
- When will employees receive equity?
- How much stock will each employee get?
- How can the company ensure that only current employees hold its stock?
- How will the plan affect the company's cash position?
- How and when will employees be able to sell their shares?
- How will current shareholders be affected?
- How can the company maximize the impact of the plan?
- How will the stock's value be determined?
- Does the plan comply with federal and state securities laws?
- How will employee-shareholders be affected if the company is sold?

DETERMINING HOW STOCK WILL BE AWARDED

Which employees will receive equity? A generation ago, equity compensation, if offered at all, was generally limited to a company's senior executive ranks. Today, led by high technology firms, many forward-looking companies in a wide range of industries issue stock or stock options to all or most of their employees. In many of these companies, the equity program is not simply "compensation," but one of the lynchpins of an organizational culture in which everyone in the firm feels invested, both financially and psychologically, in the company and its fortunes.

It is important to remember that the performance-boosting effects of equity compensation stem largely from employees' sense of belonging to a team with a common goal and shared participation in the long-term financial success of the company. In turn, team performance is greatly strengthened by open communication among the team members about those goals and incentives. When some people in the company have equity and some don't, it is more difficult to have open conversations about the growing value of the equity that pull people together and generate group energy to work for common goals. That's why many companies grant at least some equity to all personnel, even those not traditionally seen as key players, in order to create an "ownership culture."

That said, management also needs to strike a balance between all employees being focused on a common goal, and the effect of broad-based participation on the dilution of the company's ownership and the future value of the stock. In addition, while sharing equity with all employees may be important in creating a desirable culture in the organization, it is equally important to ensure that enough stock is allocated to employees to be meaningful, and to target ownership to employees who merit the award based on their contribution to enhancing the value of the company.

When will employees receive equity? In years past, the practice at many companies was to make "new hire" grants of equity—especially stock options— to employees at the time they joined the company. These grants were typically negotiated as a part of the hiring process, and were delivered as a single large grant at the commencement of employment.

This approach to granting equity has not always generated the desired results. This is due in part to the fact that the exercise price for options is generally set at the market value of the company's stock at the time the options are granted. If the company's share price later falls below the exercise price of employees' options (referred to as "underwater" options), those options may become virtually worthless to employees. Once this happens, it is often very difficult from a corporate governance perspective to amend or reissue the options at the current value. Moreover, such an amendment will typically generate further accounting charges.

In addition, one of the reasons for granting stock options is to improve employee retention, which is why grants are typically subject to a service-based vesting schedule. However, if only a single grant is made, the retentive effect of the award is substantially diluted as time passes and the award becomes vested incrementally. Multiple annual awards, rather than one-time grants, have the added benefit of layering the vesting schedule, thereby reinforcing equity compensation as a strategy to help retain employees. In addition, by making grants on a more frequent basis, it is much less likely that all the options will be underwater as a result of stock price volatility.

Allowing more frequent awards has the added benefit of rewarding employees based on actual performance. Indeed, many companies grant equity awards on a contingent basis subject to employees meeting pre-determined performance targets. This can be a particularly effective means of tying employee incentives to achieving specific corporate financial goals.

With ERISA-based plans such as ESOPs and 401(k) plans, employees are generally able to participate in the plan within one year of hire. By requiring employees to work one full year to attain eligibility to participate, short-term employees will not acquire ownership rights. These plans do not, however, permit discretionary awards based on performance, as corporate contributions to the plans are allocated based on pre-determined formulas.

How much stock will each employee get? One of the most difficult decisions for companies implementing an individual-based stock program concerns the size of the equity awards—both to individual employees and to the workforce as a whole. A decision on the size of the overall pool available for employees should begin with a return to the owner's motivation for sharing equity in the first place. For most companies, the motivation revolves around recruiting and retaining good employees, strengthening their commitment to the organization and providing them with a financial incentive based on increasing shareholder value. A decision on equity awards bounded by arbitrary parameters rather than centered on creating the most productive, high performing team will significantly reduce the effectiveness of an equity compensation program.

Decisions about the exact amount of equity to be awarded to each individual will be influenced, to a great degree, by the company's prevailing philosophy and beliefs about human resource management. Companies that subscribe to a performance-based award system may want to tailor awards of equity according to each individual's contributions to the growth of the company. Other companies believe that while performance-based awards are laudable in theory, in practice they may be flawed by a large element of subjectivity that can produce as many upset employees as inspired ones. Many companies will adopt some middle ground, awarding some of the stock by a standard formula, such as a percent of pay, with the remainder of the equity in the program reserved for special merit recognition. Many other companies (particularly companies that are publicly traded) will determine grant sizes wholly or partly based on external benchmarking data.[19] Such companies tend to consider a stock-based program

---

19 This type of approach is in effect mandated by requirements of proxy statement disclosure which compel Compensation Committees of the board to enunciate the rationale of their executive pay programs, including the role of stock-based incentives, competitive positioning and the like. Compensation Committees will often voluntarily discuss the company's overall (i.e., not just executive) compensation philosophy in their report.

as being part of the overall compensation package and determine awards based on a total compensation strategy.

The amount of ownership awarded should be financially meaningful to the employee and provide enough incentive to result in the performance the company is looking to achieve. Some companies will establish performance-based goals for equity awards. Others establish compensation goals for specific employees. These targets may either be determined on a present value basis (for example, the award should have a present value equal to 15% of base salary) or be forecasted to take into consideration the projected appreciation in the value of the company's stock at a future date as well as the aggregate value of annual grants. Note that for ERISA-based plans, the allocation of the company's contribution is determined by a formula within the plan and may not discriminate in favor of highly-compensated employees. For these plans, contributions are generally allocated pro rata to participating employees based on their annual compensation.

A company's approach to vesting will also be a factor in determining who ultimately ends up with how much of the company's equity. A long vesting schedule that requires employees to remain with the company for a substantial period of time will, in the final analysis, result in more stock being owned by those who give longer service to the company. On the other hand, an excessively long vesting requirement can be viewed with skepticism by some employees, who may feel they will never really gain permanent ownership of the stock. For ERISA-based plans, the vesting schedule may not be longer than six years.

STOCK RESTRICTIONS

How can the company ensure that only current employees hold its stock? Founding owners often have a very reasonable concern that once out of their hands, their company's stock could end up being owned by people outside the company, whether former employees or those who never were employees. This leaves entrepreneurs uneasy, fearing the possibility that an outside shareholder could cause problems for the company. While the ability of an outsider with a few shares to create a problem is, in fact, quite limited, a concern about stock passing outside of the company is legitimate, if for no other reason than it reduces the amount of equity owned by current employees. Many entrepreneurs feel a very principled commitment to the idea that the growth in the value of the company should benefit those who actively help to create it, and not former employees and other outsiders.

Fortunately, there are ways to assure that stock distributions from an employee program will remain in the hands of current employees by placing restrictions on the stock at the time it is transferred to employees. Two important restrictions for individual-based stock plans are the right of repurchase at termination and the right of first refusal.

The right of repurchase at termination gives companies the right, but not the obligation, to purchase shares from employees who terminate employment with the company. Generally, this right must be exercised at the stock's fair market value at the time of the repurchase. In many cases, these restrictions allow the company to provide employees with a note which enables the company to pay for the stock repurchase over time.

The right of first refusal gives the company the right, but not the obligation, to match any legitimate offer for the shares from outside interests. These restrictions are usually incorporated in written shareholder agreements that employees must sign at the time they are awarded equity or in the company's charter or bylaws.

It is especially important for S Corporations to include stock restrictions that give the company the right to approve any transfers of stock in order to protect the company's S Corporation status.

If a company's charter and bylaws restrict ownership to active employees, and if the company also qualifies as "substantially employee-owned" (usually at least 80% owned by active employees), the company may impose similar restrictions for shares held in qualified plans, such as ESOPs.

IMPACT ON CASH FLOW

How will the plan affect the company's cash position? Employee stock programs can take many forms that affect corporate financials differently. Some equity plans, like employee stock purchase programs and stock options, can bring cash into the company from employee purchases. Although these plans can improve cash flow, companies should not assume that employee share purchases will significantly enhance corporate cash flow. The financial effects of other equity plans may be a bit more complicated. Programs using stock grants or stock options, for example, may be roughly neutral. They require no initial cash outlay by the company in the early stages, and may even to some degree substitute for cash compensation, thus increasing the cash available to the company.

In addition, many stock plans generate current or deferred tax deductions which will decrease taxes (and therefore increase cash) without any corresponding outflow of cash to employees.

Leveraged ESOPs have a significant impact on current and future cash flows because the plan contributions are a function of the required ESOP loan repayment. Other ERISA plans using company stock, such as 401(k) or profit sharing plans, may have a positive impact on cash flow because corporate contributions of stock generate a tax deduction while preserving cash that would otherwise be used to fund employee benefits.

Whether a company adopts individual-based stock plans, such as stock purchases or options, or ERISA-based plans such as ESOPs, the requirement to provide liquidity to employee shareholders will have a negative cash flow impact in the outlying years. To plan for this financial obligation, companies should develop concrete projections that factor in the specific financial profile of the company, projections of business performance in the years ahead, and the features of the proposed equity plan. Done properly, this will provide a reasonably good estimate regarding the company's financial condition for the forecasted period.

LIQUIDITY

How and when will employees be able to sell their shares? An essential part of any employee stock ownership program is the ability of employee shareholders to sell their equity. A company establishing an employee equity program has a practical, moral and, in some cases, legal obligation to create liquidity for employee shareholders at some point.

For public companies, of course, this is not an issue since, by definition, a ready market for the company's stock is available. With ESOPs, public companies may simply issue stock to departing employees who can then sell the shares on the open market. ESOPs in closely-held companies are required by law to provide liquidity for departing ESOP participants within specified time periods (See Chapter Six for a discussion of ESOP repurchase liability requirements).

A private company that establishes an individual-based stock program will need to focus carefully on the liquidity issue when designing its plan. After all, for stock ownership to benefit the employee-shareholder, there must ultimately be a market for the shares. Not only is a reasonable liquidity mechanism a matter of fairness, but a lack of an effective strategy for providing liquidity to employee shareholders will negate the value and motivation of employee ownership.

Even though many companies hope to provide liquidity by going public or negotiating a sale or merger, for most companies this is not realistic. Liquidity expectations based on mergers or sales may be legitimate goals, but this tends to be a relatively long-term strategy. In most companies, liquidity for employee shareholders will have to be provided by the corporation itself.

Liquidity is usually not a pressing priority in the early years of the plan, since there has been insufficient time for employees to realize significant appreciation on their shares and the cost to the company to repurchase shares will be lower. It becomes more important, however, as the shares appreciate in value.

There are two main issues relative to providing liquidity for employees. A company needs to consider the cash flow implications of repurchasing stock from employees. In addition, a company should consider providing a mechanism by which employees can sell at least some of their shares while they are still employed by the company, rather than providing liquidity to employees only when they leave the company. Being able to obtain liquidity only when they leave the company may introduce a perverse incentive for employees to leave in order to cash in their ownership stake.

There are various ways for a company to provide liquidity. The simplest method is for the company to make unscheduled purchases of shares as cash flow permits. If the company can establish and fund a reserve cash account for stock repurchases, it may be possible to establish a regular schedule of stock repurchases according to a set program. Many companies establish a priority system, agreeing to repurchase shares from retiring employees first, then from employees departing prior to retirement age, then from current employees as cash permits. These repurchase programs typically include a provision allowing the company to spread the payments over a number of years, with a market rate of interest paid on amounts owed to employees.

One way to provide a high level of employee liquidity while mitigating the need for corporate repurchase of shares is to establish what is known as an internal stock market. This approach provides periodic trading opportunities at which employees can sell or buy stock as they desire. Several companies have established such mechanisms with very positive results. Contrary to what might be expected initially, these companies often receive more buy orders than sell orders from employees. This is because, in a growing company, there are many more relatively new employees (who are in a "buy" mode) than there are older employees who have reached the stage at which they desire liquidity. Rather than having to provide all of the cash to fund repurchases, companies with internal stock markets need only supply enough cash—or new shares—to balance the buy and sell orders at each trading opportunity. Note that a true internal market of the kind described here is usually viewed by the SEC as public trading, even though it is limited to employees of the company, and may require full SEC registration, though the SEC has issued "no-action" letters for companies whose internal markets meet stringent requirements for restricting the trades to transactions between employees involving only the sponsoring corporation's securities.

VOTING, DILUTION AND DISCLOSURE

How will current shareholders be affected? The decision to share equity with employees is often quite different from a decision to establish other benefit and profit sharing arrangements. Ownership goes to the heart of participation in private enterprise. Issues concerning voting rights, financial disclosure, dilution and control of the corporation are often stumbling blocks for owners of private businesses who aren't always comfortable with the idea of sharing ownership and information with other shareholders, even within their organization.

Voting

When employees own stock directly, they have the right to vote their shares on all matters that require a shareholder vote, including election of the board of directors. In some cases, it may be possible to use non-voting stock, but not allowing employees to have all the rights that go with ownership may defeat the purpose of sharing ownership—having employees who think and act like owners.

Voting rules for shareholders are governed by a company's charter and by the state where it is incorporated. Each state has different rules regarding voting, although shareholders generally vote on the following issues:

- Election or removal of the board of directors.
- Adoption or amendment of the company's bylaws.
- Merger or consolidation of the corporation with another company.
- Transfer of substantially all of the property (assets) of the company.
- Voluntary dissolution of the company.
- Required additional capital investments by shareholders.
- Substantial change in corporate structure.
- Approval of the company's auditor.

There are various ways to address concerns regarding voting of shares. Non-voting shares can be used in some instances to mitigate the dilution of voting control or, in the case of qualified plans in private companies, voting of the shares (for most issues) can be controlled by the trustee of the plan who can be an insider of the company. In some plans, such as ESOPs, employees must be given pass-through voting rights to direct the trustee on major corporate issues such as mergers, acquisitions and sale of substantially all of the company's assets. The Department of Labor and the IRS require the trustee in all cases to vote the shares in the best financial interests of plan participants. In rare instances, this may require the trustee to override the voting directions of the plan participants. Some corporations choose to allow employees to vote on corporate issues even when it is not legally required. In public companies, voting rights on allocated shares must be passed through to ESOP participants on all issues.

Dilution

Sharing stock ownership with employees causes shareholders to incur dilution of their ownership percentage. It is important, however, for owners to distinguish between "percentage" dilution and "economic" dilution, and to fully understand all of the ownership and economic impacts of the plan. Owners often express concern if their ownership percentage decreases, when in reality the economic value of their ownership may increase if the company's performance improves as a result of the stock program. Employees should be offered ownership with the intention that the added incentive it provides will create greater overall company value and thus greater value for all shareholders than if no equity was shared.

To determine the amount of dilution that may result from an equity sharing program, it is useful to develop an ownership-forecasting model. Using different corporate growth and stock allocation assumptions, such a model can help companies determine how much stock dilution is reasonable while still allowing for a satisfactory return on equity for current shareholders.

The sample model presented below incorporates certain assumptions concerning corporate growth rates, company share value, the number and growth rates of participating employee groups at various levels of the organization, their average salaries, and the targeted equity values for each employee group. Incorporated in an interactive spreadsheet, such a model allows for experimentation with varying award levels to help determine the appropriate balance between the incentives made available to employees and the resulting dilution of current shareholders, while also factoring in the effects of various company · growth assumptions.

The following assumptions are used in this example:
- The company is initially capitalized with 1,000,000 shares outstanding.
- The company's current value is $1,000,000 and grows 100% per year for the first 3 years.
- At end of year 3, the company employs 2 senior employees at an average salary of $100,000, 4 middle management employees at an average salary of $60,000, and 25 other employees at an average salary of $35,000.
- Targeted ownership compensation levels at end of year 3 are 300% of annual compensation for senior employees, 100% for middle management and 50% for other employees.

Assuming the projected growth rate and employment levels bear out, this owner will be able to achieve the desired equity compensation targets by making just 16% of the company's stock available to employees. Even though this will dilute his ownership from 75% to 63%, the value of his ownership is projected to grow from $750,000 to over $5 million. Based on this model, it would be recommended that the owner reserve 20% of the company's equity for the employee ownership program.

Ownership Forecasting Model

Start—Year 1

	Shares	% of Ownership	Value	Multiple of Salaries
Owner	750,000	75%	$750,000	N/A
Investors	250,000	25%	$250,000	N/A
Senior Employees				0
Middle Management				0
Other Employees				0
Price per Share			$1.00	
Total Employee Ownership		0%		

End of Year 3

	Shares	% of Ownership	Total Value	Number of Employees	Multiple of Salaries (per employee)
Owner	750,000	63%	$5,040,000		N/A
Investors	250,000	21%	$1,680,000		N/A
Senior Employees	89,285	7.5%	$600,000	2	300%
Middle Management	35,714	3.0%	$240,000	4	100%
Other Employees	65,104	5.5%	$437,500	25	50%
Price per Share			$6.72		
Total Employee Ownership		16%			

Financial Disclosure

Financial disclosure is another concern of many business owners. Shareholder rights to receive information differ for companies whose securities are registered with the SEC versus privately held companies. Publicly traded companies must periodically disclose financial information to their stockholders. For a private company, the state in which it is incorporated and the registration or exemption requirements for the particular plan being used will determine the amount of information that must be given to employee shareholders. In many states, a private company is not legally required to give shareholders regular financial information.

With regard to qualified plans such as ESOPs, federal regulations require that employees receive a summary plan description and annual statements as to the value of their personal account in the plan and the value of the shares of employer securities within the plan.

Private corporations need to balance these minimum standards against the goal of having employees sufficiently understand the operations of the business in order to help improve corporate performance. Without knowing and understanding some measures of financial performance, employees will have little ability to judge the impact of their efforts on overall corporate performance. To provide employees with the ability to measure the effectiveness of their efforts, sales and profitability figures should be communicated to employees including, if possible, further breakdowns of income and costs by business division. Ideally, employees should be able to see how their own contribution impacts the company's bottom line.

COMMUNICATIONS

How can the company maximize the impact of the plan? By the time an entrepreneur implements an employee equity plan, he typically has a good understanding of how the program works and the value it may represent to the participating employees.

However, it is easy to forget that the typical employee does not share this knowledge. When the entrepreneur announces that the company now has an employee ownership program, many employees, even those with advanced education, have only a vague idea of what it means.

Employee stock ownership can build strong loyalty and commitment, motivate performance, energize the workforce and promote entrepreneurial attitudes within the organization. For that to happen, however, the organization will first have to attend to the critical issues of communication, financial information sharing and employee participation. If employee stock ownership is the seed, then communication is the water and employee participation is the means of tilling the garden. Only by combining the incentive of ownership with effective employee communications and participation programs will a high level of business performance bloom.

What exactly do employees need to understand? At the outset, five things are fundamental:
- What is stock?
- How does the equity program work?
- How does the program affect them?
- What determines the value of their stock?
- What can they do to help increase the value of the stock over time?

Each of these components is critical, but having employees understand how value is created will ultimately have the greatest impact on the bottom line. Employees should understand that the value of their equity will be determined primarily by the company's net earnings. The more profit the company generates, the more valuable its stock will be. By making a focus on company profits part of the fabric of the organization, employees will be able to understand exactly how their work affects the company's earnings. This understanding, known as "line of sight," becomes a powerful force for improved business results.

How does the process of training and education get carried out? Be warned: it's not easy. And it is not something that can be done just once. After all, new employees will be brought on and each will need to be educated about the company's stock plan. Even current employees may need a refresher from time to time on how they can affect the company's success.

Creating An Ownership Culture

Ownership is a powerful notion, implying as it does a whole packet of rights and responsibilities. A company that wants to take ownership seriously needs to define what ownership means in the context of their company and help everyone in the organization understand it. The challenge is to make ownership *real* in ways to enable employees to think and act like owners.

A key principle associated with creating an ownership culture starts with the premise that employees will actually be owners. That means that they must have an opportunity to acquire equity incentives in amounts sufficient to provide meaningful financial benefits, and that ownership awards are not simply a one-off opportunity but part of an ongoing incentive program.

In addition to an active and ongoing education and communication program about the stock plan, companies wanting to implement an ownership culture need to educate their employees about the company itself. Optimally, this would include an approach known as "open book management," where employees are educated not only about the key financial drivers of company value but also how they can help improve overall operations to improve shareholder value.

Successful ownership cultures blend a variety of dynamics. The companies that get the most from employee ownership use communications, information sharing and employee participation combined with programs that empower employees to take initiative in solving problems and producing creative ideas. These efforts help to distinguish high-performance companies from their competitors.

Broad-based employee ownership can change employees' expectations, challenging them to think and operate differently in terms of their relative position within a corporate environment. An ownership culture changes the employer-employee relationship and creates new challenges and opportunities for managers and employees alike. Every company looking to establish an ownership culture has to devise its own approaches to defining the roles and responsibilities of employee-owners to create a different kind of workplace that maximizes the power of ownership.

Research strongly suggests that those companies that combine substantial employee ownership incentives with participatory workplaces that enable employees to truly think and act like owners can achieve statistically significant performance improvement. The payoff for both the company and its employees can be substantial but it requires a commitment of the company's leadership to invest the time and effort required to make the most of an ownership culture.

VALUATION

How will the stock's value be determined? Everyone involved in an employee stock program, from founding owners to participating employees, will want to know just what the company's stock is worth and how the value is determined. For public companies, the answer is straightforward: the stock price is established through the public stock market and its value is published every day in the news media. For privately held companies, however, no such yardstick exists.

If a private company is establishing an ESOP, the rules in this area are also straightforward: ultimate responsibility for determining the fair market value of the stock lies with the plan's fiduciaries, but to meet this responsibility, they are required by law to obtain the opinion of a well-qualified, independent valuation firm.

For stock option and other non-ESOP plans, the company's board of directors has the responsibility to determine in good faith the fair market value of the company's stock. The term "good faith" means that the board of directors must honestly and reasonably believe that the value they assign to the stock is a good approximation of its actual fair market value. Ultimately, it is the Internal Revenue Service (or in the case of litigation, a court) that will determine whether a board of directors has met this good faith standard. In addition, under the new accounting standards for stock-based compensation, certain attributes of the company or the stock, such as class of the shares, can or should be taken into account in valuing the shares of private companies. Accordingly, it is important that the valuation process meet both minimum tax and accounting standards.

Approaches to Determining Fair Market Value

The "gold standard" for determining fair market value is to retain the services of a professional valuation firm. However, a company can also meet IRS standards for a good faith determination of fair market value by applying a formula (which may be developed in consultation with a professional appraiser or may be developed by the company's in-house financial staff) that is designed to produce a reasonable estimate of value.

Whether a company determines the fair market value of its stock on its own or retains the services of a professional appraiser, its board should be familiar with the commonly used approaches to the task. There are a number of valuation methodologies that have traditionally been used by investment bankers and business appraisers. These include capitalization of earnings, discounted cash flow, comparable sales, industry rules-of-thumb, and asset valuation. Each of these approaches is discussed below.

- **Capitalization Approach.** Capitalization of earnings is an approach that involves the application of a multiple, or "price-to-earnings ratio," to the company's earnings or cash flow. For publicly traded companies, the price-to-earnings or price-to-cash flow ratio is as straightforward as its name sounds: the price of the stock divided by the earnings or cash flow of the company. In applying this approach to a private company, appropriate capitalization rates (or multiples) are generally based on the price-to-earnings ratios of the stock of comparable publicly traded companies. These ratios are derived by dividing the stock price of the comparable public company by its earnings or cash flows. These comparables are then applied to the private company's current or projected earnings and cash flows to derive an overall valuation projection. To better refine the process, the data for the comparable public companies are adjusted to reflect the difference in the size, profitability, leverage, liquidity, operating characteristics and other factors of those companies as compared to the company being valued.

- **Discounted Cash Flow Approach.** A basic premise of economics is that a dollar in hand today is more valuable than a dollar that will be received tomorrow. The discounted cash flow (DCF) approach applies this concept (known as "present value") to determine the value of a company.

  Using the DCF approach, an appraiser will estimate the future earnings of the company over the next several years as well as the market value of the company at the end of that span of years, referred to for DCF purposes as the "terminal value." The appraiser will then determine the present value of the projected earnings and terminal value. To do so, he will "discount" those projected values based on several factors, including the currently prevailing rate of return available on other investments as well as the risk that the company may fail to produce the projected earnings.

- **Comparable Sales.** In pricing a house for sale, the homeowner looks to the surrounding neighborhood to examine the prices at which comparable houses have sold. In comparing sale prices, the homeowner would make "adjustments" for the differences in the features of his house relative to the comparable houses. For example, all other things being equal, a higher value would be placed on a home in a quiet location than on a busy street.

  A similar approach can be applied to determine the value of a company. The appraiser would assess comparable sales within the industry, being careful to determine whether the transaction was conducted at arm's-length, representing an accurate reflection of fair market value. Next, the appraiser would analyze the specific terms of the sale, including non-compete agreements and seller financing, among others.

- **Industry Rules-of-Thumb.** Many industries have a traditional "rule-of-thumb" by which company values are often measured, such as five times pre-tax earnings, or two times book value. These rules-of-thumb, however, are seldom valid in and of themselves for determining a company's value. A basic problem with them is that they are a static indication of value. Investors' assessments of value, by contrast, are ever-changing, making true market value dynamic in nature.

- **Asset Approaches.** In general, there are two types of asset approaches: going-concern and liquidation. A going-concern approach expresses value as a function of the company's book value. This approach may be useful for businesses with substantial tangible assets where recent earnings do not reflect the company's intrinsic value. Liquidation approaches are used when the company is better off "dead than alive."

In order to retain latitude and flexibility, an equity-sharing plan should not specify the exact approach that will be used to determine the fair market value of the company's stock. Instead, the plan (assuming that it is a non-ERISA plan) should simply state that the stock's fair market value will be determined by the company's board of directors. The board can then adopt an internal policy on how it will determine the company's share price, which it will be able to change when warranted without having to formally amend the plan documents. As part of the company's employee communications efforts, it should be clarified for the employees exactly how the company's share price will be determined.

Valuing Equity in Deferred Compensation Plans

Proposed regulations for Internal Revenue Code Section 409A governing deferred compensation plans set forth specific guidelines for valuing deferred compensation programs based on the use of employer stock. While not all equity compensation arrangements are subject to Section 409A,[20] deferred compensation arrangements must generally follow guidelines in the 409A regulations for determining the fair market value (FMV) of the stock.

For public companies whose stock is readily tradable on an established securities market, FMV is the last sale price before or the first sale price after the grant, the closing selling price on the grant date or the immediately preceding trading day, or any other reasonable basis using actual transactions. It is also permissible to utilize an average selling price over a specified period within 30 days before or 30 days after the grant if the number and value of the equity units are fixed prior to the averaging period and such valuation method is used consistently for all grants under the program.

For closely-held companies whose stock is not traded on an established exchange, FMV must be established by the reasonable application of a reasonable valuation method. Factors to be taken into account to meet the reasonableness standard must include the value of the tangible and intangible assets of the corporation, the present value of future cash flows, the market value of stock or equity interests in similar corporations or entities engaged in substantially the same business, and other relevant factors such as control premiums or minority discounts. All available information material to the corporation must be considered.

The consistent use of an independent appraiser within 12 months of the grant date or a consistently applied valuation formula based on the tax principles governing the valuation of shares subject to non-lapse restrictions, which must be consistently applied for all purposes, will be afforded a presumption of reasonableness for purposes of the Section 409A valuation standards.

For an illiquid stock not subject to any non-lapse put or call right or obligation (other than a right of first refusal) and issued by a start-up corporation that is less than 10 years old, a written valuation report that takes into account the above-referenced factors and is prepared by a person with significant knowledge and experience or training in performing similar valuations is acceptable.

---

20 Incentive stock options (ISOs), Section 423 stock purchase plans, non-qualified stock options (NSOs) with an exercise price no less than fair market value as of the grant date, and certain stock appreciation rights (SARs) may be exempted from 409A under certain conditions.

SECURITIES REGISTRATION

Does the plan comply with federal and state securities laws? Following the stock market crash of 1929, major legislation was enacted on both the federal and state levels to reform the securities markets and to provide certain protections to investors. On the federal level, this reform movement led to the creation of the Securities and Exchange Commission (SEC) to regulate the issuance and trading of securities, and the activities of securities exchanges and those who work in the securities industry. In addition, most states enacted their own securities laws, sometimes called "Blue Sky" laws, which differ from federal law and from one state to another. In some cases, Blue Sky laws impose even stricter standards than federal securities laws.

Generally, a company cannot offer or sell its securities to the public unless it has first registered those securities with the SEC. The registration process requires the company to supply initial and ongoing comprehensive business and financial information for public disclosure to provide potential investors a clear picture of the risks involved in purchasing the company's securities. Registration of securities with the SEC and the various states can be time consuming and quite expensive. However, a number of exemptions from the registration process are available. A private company developing an equity compensation program involving the sale of securities to employees will want to retain a qualified attorney to determine if the planned program qualifies for one of the available exemptions.

Exemptions from Securities Registration

The first question that must be addressed in this area is whether the planned equity compensation program involves the offer and sale of securities. Stock compensation in the form of grants are not considered to involve the sale of securities and therefore would not fall within the scope of federal securities registration requirements in most instances. Contributions to ERISA-regulated employee benefit plans (such as ESOPs) are specifically exempted from federal securities regulation. By contrast, stock option and stock purchase plans are generally considered to involve an offer of securities for sale and would fall within the scope of the federal securities registration laws.

Once it has been determined that a program involves the sale of securities, the next question is whether exemptions from securities registration requirements are available. There are several possible exemptions. Whether a company qualifies for a specific exemption generally depends on how many people will purchase the securities, how sophisticated the purchasers are as investors, how much money will be raised from the sale of securities, the manner in which information will be given to the investors and the contents of that information. Some of the common federal securities registration exemptions include:

- **Raising less than $1 million.** If the company sells less than $1 million worth of its securities in a 12-month period, a federal exemption may be available provided the company has not issued other securities in reliance on certain other exemptions and the company did not engage in a general solicitation to find the investors (which should not pose a problem in the case of offerings restricted to employees).

- **Sales of up to $5 million.** If a company raises no more than $5 million from the sale of its securities in a 12-month period, it may sell its securities without SEC registration to an unlimited number of "accredited" investors and up to 35 non-accredited investors provided that the company supplies the investors with certain business and financial information required by the securities laws and does not engage in a general solicitation. Accredited investors include the company's directors and executive officers and others whose individual net worth exceeds $1 million or whose annual income exceeds $200,000 for the previous two years (or $300,000 when including the joint income from a spouse) and is expected to exceed the same level in the current year.

- **Sales of securities in excess of $5 million.** If the amount of capital raised by a company in a 12-month period from integrated issuances of securities exceeds $5 million, it may sell securities without SEC registration to an unlimited number of accredited investors and up to 35 non-accredited investors. The main difference for sales of more than $5 million compared to sales of up to $5 million is that more substantial and detailed information on the company and its operations will have to be furnished to the investors, and each non-accredited investor must be a sophisticated investor or be assisted by a purchaser representative who is a sophisticated investor.

- **Sales of securities to investors who all live in the same state.** There is a rarely used federal exemption for securities sold by a company having all of its investors residing in the same state. This exemption requires the company to conduct its business operations and be incorporated in the same state where all of its investors reside. Sometimes referred to as the "coffee shop rule," this exemption requires careful planning and strict execution.

- **SEC Rule 701.** This rule provides a limited exemption intended expressly for securities sold as part of an equity compensation program. This exemption is not available to companies required to file quarterly and annual reports with the SEC, but can be an attractive mechanism for small, closely held corporations interested in implementing a stock option plan or an employee stock purchase plan. Under Rule 701, stock may be offered for sale to a company's employees, directors, general partners, trustees, officers or consultants under a written compensatory benefit plan. Under Rule 701, a company cannot, in any one 12-month period, sell securities worth more than (a) $1,000,000, (b) 15% of the total assets of the issuer or (c) 15% of the total number of outstanding securities of the class being issued based on this exemption. It is important to note that with respect to stock options, the time of sale is considered to be the option grant date and their value is equal to their exercise price.[21] The issuer is required to furnish a copy of the compensatory benefit plan to each employee investor, and, in cases where the company raises more than $5 million in any 12-month period, the issuer must provide the employee investors with additional financial information about the issuer and the risks involved in investing in the securities. Unlike other exemptions, securities offered under Rule 701 are not subject to integration with other exempt offerings.

- **Regulation S.** If a company has overseas facilities, it may want to issue its securities to its non-U.S. employees. Regulation S may permit the company to offer and sell its securities in offshore transactions without registration, but cannot be used to stimulate U.S. market interest in the securities sold overseas. It is important to note that Regulation S does not include the dollar value and non-accredited investor limitations found in other exemptions.

The exemptions discussed above (other than the intra-state sales exemption) are safe harbors designed to help companies structure their stock programs with confidence that securities sold according to these rules do not require registration. Other offers and sales may not require registration provided they do not involve a public distribution. No "bright line" test exists defining when a company makes a public distribution. Because the facts and circumstances of each offering will vary and will determine whether an exemption is available, companies should consult a qualified securities attorney before executing an investment plan.

It is important to remember that, in addition to qualifying for an exemption from the federal securities registration laws, the company needs to determine whether it qualifies for an exemption from registration in each state in which the company or any of its investors (including employee investors) reside. Although some of these state Blue Sky laws contain exemptions which mirror some of the federal exemptions discussed above, they may still review the merits of a particular offering. New York State, for example, requires the companies themselves to register rather than registering the securities being issued. Even if an exemption

---

21 So a grant of 150,000 options on shares having a current strike price and value of $10 each would have a value of $1,500,000.

from registration exists under state law, the company may still have to file a notice of sale with and pay a small fee to the state securities authority. Blue Sky law compliance can be time consuming and expensive if a company has shareholders residing in a large number of states. However, for large companies whose stock is traded on a national securities market, federal law prohibits the states from requiring these listed companies to register their securities with individual state securities commissions.

Companies must always comply with federal and state anti-fraud laws when issuing securities even if an exemption from registration is available. Written and oral disclosure about the company and its securities must be accurate and complete, and may not be misleading due to any omissions. As a result, it is advisable for companies to restrict disclosure to written materials, instruct their officers and employees not to make oral representations, inform investors that no company representative is authorized to make oral disclosures to investors and deliver written business and financial information to investors (both accredited and non-accredited), even if not required to obtain the benefit of a registration exemption.

Companies should understand that the exemptions discussed in this section are available only to issuers of securities. Once the company's securities are held by investors, the investors cannot resell them without registering the resale unless a different exemption is available. In other words, securities issued based on exemption from registration are restricted securities. Other safe harbors exist that enable securities holders to resell their securities in limited amounts over certain periods of time.

EMPLOYEE OWNERSHIP AS AN EXIT STRATEGY

How will employee-shareholders be affected if the company is sold? Whether or not an entrepreneur currently has a sale of the company in mind, it is important to recognize how the company's stock program, and therefore the employees' ownership interests, would be affected should the company be sold. Relative to employee stock programs, the term for a sale of the company, which may appear in the plan's legal documents, is "change of control."

In the case of an ESOP, an acquirer will typically want to buy full ownership of the company, including the shares owned by the ESOP. The decision on whether or not to sell the shares owned by an ESOP is a fiduciary one, and must be made by the trustee(s), subject to ERISA fiduciary standards. For a sale of substantially all of the assets of the corporation, the ESOP trustee would be obligated to allow employees to direct the voting of the shares held in their respective ESOP accounts. If the trustee accepts the offer to buy the ESOP shares, the money paid by the acquirer will be allocated to the employees' ESOP accounts in place of the shares that were formerly in those accounts. If the ESOP was leveraged and still has an acquisition loan outstanding (and therefore has stock in the ESOP suspense account), the proceeds from the sale of the stock in the suspense account will be used to pay off the balance of the loan, with any remaining money then allocated to employee accounts. Following the sale and allocation of proceeds as described above, the ESOP will likely be terminated by the acquiring owner, with the employees rolling over the cash from their ESOP accounts to IRA accounts or other qualified plans such as a 401(k).

Accelerated Vesting

In the case of a stock option plan, the main issue regarding a change of control is whether or not a "vesting acceleration" provision is included in the plan. With a provision of this kind in place, employees who have been granted options, but have not yet met the length of service requirements to become fully vested, would nevertheless be treated as fully vested in the event of a change of control.

Typically, the acquisition of one company by another will result in some employees of the acquired company being laid off. Ironically, very often these are the same personnel who had to work extra hard during the transition period to facilitate the deal. If no vesting acceleration provision were included in the plan, these employees would forfeit their unvested options when laid off.

There are advantages and disadvantages to including a vesting acceleration provision in the plan. Many argue that individual based stock plans should provide for accelerated vesting in the event of a change of control, thereby assuring that employees who may get laid off will not be harmed by the transaction. Others believe that a plan should not provide accelerated vesting because it may make the company less attractive to the acquirer. The concern is that if the employees can exercise all their options upon acquisition of the company and then sell their stock, they may do just that and then resign, leaving the newly combined company without key staff. An acquiring company would therefore prefer that unvested options remain as an incentive for employees to stay on with the new company.

Fortunately, there is a way to "have your cake and eat it too." A stock option plan can contain a provision that grants accelerated vesting only if the employee is laid off within a specified time—say, 12 months—following a change of control. This approach protects employees who are laid off while retaining incentives to encourage other employees to remain with the new company.

Tag-Along and Drag-Along Rights

Another issue can arise when the primary shareholder wants to accept a purchase offer for the company but minority shareholders (whether employee shareholders or other minority investors) are involved. One variation of this problem occurs when the acquiring company wants to own 100 % of the target company's stock but the minority shareholders are not willing to sell. Another variation occurs when the acquiring company is interested in buying only the controlling interest of the primary shareholder, leaving the minority shareholders out of the deal. These possibilities can be addressed through the creation of a stockholders' agreement that is adopted in connection with an employee stock plan. Such an agreement can establish what are sometimes referred to as "tag-along" and "drag-along" rights. These stipulate that the majority shareholder cannot accept an offer to purchase his shares unless the offer has been made to all shareholders, and that if the majority shareholder agrees to a sale or merger of the company, all of the shareholders can be required to tender their shares to the acquirer at the same share price and on the same terms and conditions.

SPECIAL TAX ISSUES FOR EMPLOYEE OWNERSHIP PROGRAMS IN S CORPORATIONS AND LLCs

Shareholders of S Corporations and members of LLCs are taxed as if they were members of a partnership. As such, all of the current income or losses of the S Corporation or LLC are attributed to the shareholders/members, even though they may not receive any actual distribution of earnings. As a result of this attribution of earnings, employee owners of S Corporations and LLCs will be required to personally pay tax on the corporate-level earnings. Income attributed to employees has the same character for tax purposes as it does at the underlying entity. Accordingly, employees will be deemed to have earned their proportionate share of ordinary income and realized capital gains or losses.

In most cases, cash distributions are made to shareholders/members to enable them to pay the taxes on this attributed income. This increased level of income may disentitle the employees to certain income-based tax credits or deductions, or affect the itemized deductions that can be claimed on their tax returns. It is not possible to fully anticipate the tax implications of such deemed income for a broad employee base. As the taxation of partnerships is fairly complex, special efforts should be made to educate employees on how to file their income tax returns properly.

There are also complexities relating to how an employee's cost base (for capital gains purposes) of his interest in the S Corporation or LLC is calculated. Generally speaking, an employee's cost base in his shares of an S Corporation or membership interest in an LLC is equal to what he paid for it. The cost base will be increased by income attributed to him and decreased (but never below zero) by distributions paid or losses attributed to him. In addition, if the employee obtained his interest in the S Corporation or LLC by way of stock grant or stock option, he will be required to include in income (as ordinary income) the difference between the value of the stock on the date of vesting or acquisition, as the case may be, less whatever he paid for it.[22] This taxable benefit is also added to the cost base of the employee's shares in the S Corporation or interest in the LLC.

The increase in value of the company, as represented by its share value, may also be subject to a gain if the actual business of the company is sold via an asset sale. It is therefore possible that the employee will, in effect, be subject to tax twice on the same gain. Where an asset sale occurs, the gain will be computed at the organization level, and then attributed to the employee in the year of sale. The gain computed at the corporate level will generally be larger than the gain the employee will realize on his shares, since it is computed by reference to the corporation's historical cost basis. This attributed gain will increase the employee's cost base. If the employee then surrenders his shares in the same year for a distribution of the proceeds from the sale, this will typically generate an offsetting capital loss. However, the employee's cost base will generally be much higher than the proceeds distributed, so he will generally realize a capital loss that cannot be utilized to offset the ordinary income realized when he acquired the shares via the exercise of a stock option or through the vesting of restricted stock. Moreover, to the extent that any of the gain on the asset sale was treated as ordinary income and not capital gain (which commonly occurs to some extent in asset sales), the employee will not be able to set the capital loss off against this ordinary income attributed to him, so he may be subject to an unexpected and potentially significant tax bill.

Accordingly, if there is a reasonable likelihood that the business carried on by an S Corporation or LLC will be sold via an asset sale (which is typically how purchasers prefer to structure these transactions), it is very important to address these potentially deleterious tax issues at the time the program is implemented and probably restrict the program only to senior management, who should obtain personal tax advice prior to participating in the program. A phantom stock or SAR plan may work best for broad-based programs in these entities.

---

22 Unless the option is exercised early for "unvested shares" and an 83(b) election was made, in which case the amount to be included in income may be reduced or eliminated. See Chapter Two for a discussion of Section 83(b) elections.

Chapter Twelve

Getting the Most from Employee Ownership

For entrepreneurs, the most exciting aspect of employee ownership is its potential to raise a company's level of business performance. A workforce of employees who hold a real financial interest in the fortunes of the enterprise conjures up visions of an organization in which people show dedication, take responsibility, put in extra effort, boost productivity, cut waste, delight customers and generate a bigger bottom line.

Employee ownership can indeed lead to those results. Dramatic examples abound of companies that have pushed performance to unprecedented levels by taking the employee ownership path. But just as many examples can be cited of companies that gained little from employee ownership. In fact, a series of research studies has confirmed what Beyster Institute experts know from experience: *simply adopting an employee ownership plan is by itself unlikely to improve business performance.*

The truth is, if you put in an employee stock plan, but then go back to business as usual, you will get the usual results. The million dollar question, then, is this: What exactly does it take to unlock the powerful potential of employee ownership to raise business performance? What changes are needed to produce the desired results?

Decades of experience with employee ownership have produced some convincing answers. The first step is to understand companies that *have* been successful in using employee ownership as a springboard to better performance. These organizations are characterized by different attitudes, behaviors, roles and responsibilities compared to most conventional companies. At companies that simply consult with a lawyer, draw up an employee stock plan, and then send out a memo or hold a meeting notifying the employees that they are now the legal beneficiaries of, say, a "tax-qualified defined contribution employee stock ownership arrangement pursuant to Section 401(a) of the Internal Revenue Code and ERISA," those changes in attitudes, behaviors, etc. just don't happen.

YOU "GOTTA WANNA"

The fact is that at most companies, the workforce doesn't respond with transformed performance levels because they don't fully understand the whole picture of what is happening and the special opportunity it represents for them. And it's not their fault. Very few employees indeed have acquired the level of knowledge—either from the schools or from their employer—that is needed to grasp exactly what it means to own an equity interest in a company—especially with the added complication of doing it through a company-sponsored employee ownership program.

Why does an entrepreneur feel so passionately about the fortunes of his company? For most, there are two reasons. First, it represents an opportunity to create wealth for himself and his family, with all the security and opportunity that wealth can bring. Second, he harbors a strong feeling of pride in what he is able to accomplish—the business is his "baby" and if it is successful he can enjoy deep satisfaction and pride of accomplishment.

For an employee ownership program to become a catalyst for improved business performance, the employees, too, must come to really care about the fortunes of the company. Without the core sense of motivation that comes from really caring about the outcome, the idea that employees will boost business performance is wishful thinking. As Jack Stack, the remarkably effective president of employee-owned Springfield Remanufacturing, Inc. puts it, "you gotta wanna."

HANDING OVER THE KEYS

Then there is a second problem. Even if employees grasp the nature of the opportunity that is being made available to them and come to really care about the success of the business, the company may only nibble at the full potential of employee ownership. The problem is that conventional companies are structured and operated in a way that is designed for a workforce of people who *don't* really care about the ultimate success of the company. These structures and operating systems rarely provide employees with much latitude to use their own creativity and judgment, nor do they equip employees with the information and skills beyond what is directly necessary to carry out narrow, structured roles and tasks. As a result, employee-owners who embrace their status as co-owners and grasp the special opportunity it affords may find that they have limited ability and opportunity to act on their new-found motivation. They may understand that if the company increases its market value, they stand to reap a valuable financial gain, but they don't know what factors actually drive company value and cause it to increase—and if they did, they wouldn't know how to effectively impact those factors.

The highly successful employee ownership companies empower employee-owners by really teaching them the business they are in. They provide the business training and ongoing access to information that people need to stay on top of what's going on. Once motivated employee-owners understand how the game is played, they can at last become truly proactive and effective in producing better results.

OWNERSHIP CULTURE

Among employee ownership companies, this aspect of their operations, in which employee-owners are "in the know" and engaged in driving the performance of the business with passion and personal initiative, has come to be known as "ownership culture." It reflects a different set of expectations within the company about roles and responsibilities. Like two sides of one coin, employee-owners have more expected *of* them and more expected *by* them. They must be: more conscientious, more productive, more innovative, more responsible, more proactive, more customer-oriented. At the same time, they must receive: more information, more say, more latitude, more room for personal judgment, more respect, more dignity.

Companies develop their own particular style when it comes to creating their ownership culture, the variations reflecting the values and personality of their leaders and their people. While the styles vary, the fundamental issues that are consistently addressed by high-performing employee ownership companies are remarkably consistent. Here we will touch on four important elements that companies should consider as they implement their equity compensation program:

- **Provide Enough Ownership to Matter.** This is really more of a pre-condition to building an effective ownership culture than an element of the culture itself, but it is too important to leave unsaid. Very simply, the financial opportunity that is being made available to employees must be significant enough to justify to the employee the kind of extra effort that will come to be expected of him. Token or symbolic awards of a few shares will not be effective. How much it takes to get an employee to "sit up and take notice" will vary with each individual. Executives who already enjoy high levels of compensation and may have opportunities to jump ship for lucrative recruiting offers may require considerably larger ownership interests than a line employee whose expectations are more modest. The bottom line is that each employee must feel that the opportunity being offered is a special one that justifies a personal commitment.

- **Teach Everyone the Business.** Employee owners need to understand the company's business, what factors affect company performance, and how company success is measured. To be fully effective, employee-owners need to understand the elements that appear on income statements and balance sheets.

- **Share Real Time Information on Business Performance.** It is important to keep employee-owners informed about how the company is progressing in meeting goals. If they are unaware of problems, they can't be expected to fix them.

- **Continuous Improvement of Operating Processes.** Everyone in the business must apply their insights and creativity toward creating more effective ways to operate. Employee ownership companies that have seen a substantial jump in their performance have gotten there by re-thinking and re-tooling how they do things, eliminating layers of supervision, adding responsibilities to front line people, and finding efficiencies small and large in everything they do. They end up with levels of productivity that conventional competitors simply cannot match.

IT'S A WIN-WIN SITUATION

The benefits of an employee ownership culture are substantial, beginning with the opportunity for business success. A company that taps the full potential of employee ownership to boost productivity and business performance gains a major competitive advantage. Over the long term, this advantage can lead to tremendous growth, a leading industry position and substantial financial returns. Along with that comes the great sense of accomplishment, pride and self-esteem that comes with having built a business that succeeds in a big way.

But there is more than business success to be gained. At the Beyster Institute, we have often had conversations with entrepreneurs who have built strong programs of employee ownership and culture. Regularly, these individuals comment on how the employee ownership strategy has made their lives better. They often express appreciation that so many others are there to take on responsibility for the success of the business. The ability to delegate so much of the leader's burden is highly valued. As one such entrepreneur said, "I used to be in the office until all hours of the night. But now that my people are taking so much responsibility and initiative, I get to go home at 5:00 and have dinner with my wife. I really value that."

Entrepreneurs also tell us of the satisfaction they find in seeing the people in their company grow and develop as individuals. We hear of employees that joined the company with little more than a high school diploma and a willingness to work and who then flourished in the empowered environment of an ownership culture. Many entrepreneurs take heart in seeing such people develop their talents, grow professionally, contribute to the organization and build highly successful lives with a level of financial security for themselves and their families that they could not have approached working at a conventional company.

Equity sharing offers benefits that are unparalleled. A company with engaged employees that are committed to the business, exhibit a sense of shared responsibility, and have a stake in the outcome has a chance at real success, and employees and owners alike have an opportunity for personal and financial growth.

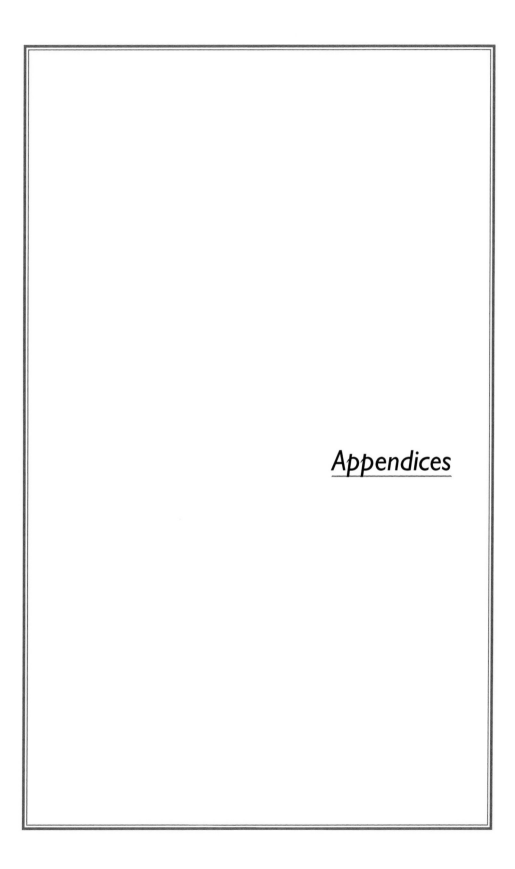

Appendices

Business Legal Form and the Equity Sharing Decision

Business organizations in the U.S. can operate in any of several alternative legal forms, including sole proprietorship, general partnership, limited partnership, limited liability partnership (LLP), limited liability company (LLC) and, of course, the stock corporation, which may be of the S Corporation variety or the more standard C Corporation.[23] The legal form actually chosen by a business will determine, to a great degree, which type of equity sharing arrangement may be suitable for the company.

The most important differences among the various forms generally center on four factors:

- Tax consequences.
- Exposure to legal liability.
- Management or governance.
- Transferability of ownership interests (ability to sell).

The following briefly discusses the most common business forms and their effect upon equity compensation strategy.

GENERAL PARTNERSHIPS

A partnership is an association of two or more persons (there is no limit on the number) who carry on a business as co-owners. Ownership interests are defined by contractual agreements among the owners. A number of variations on this theme

---

23 While these are the major forms of business entity, there are numerous other specialized forms, such as the mutual insurance company, the real estate investment trust (REIT) and the regulated investment company (RIC or mutual fund).

exist, known by names such as syndicate, joint venture or unincorporated organization. State law recognizes a partnership as a separate entity from its owners, so the assets of a partnership will be held in the name of the partnership, rather than by the owners directly. For tax purposes, however, a partnership is a "pass-through" entity. Although a partnership must generally file its own tax return, all income or loss generated by the partnership is assigned to the partners. The partners also bear personal liability for the debts of the partnership. A business owned as a partnership is managed by its partners, although the partners are free to appoint one or more partners as the managing partners. Because ownership is determined by contractual agreements, transferability of ownership is greatly restricted and is generally not possible (except upon death) without the consent of all partners, or as permitted and determined by the governing partnership agreements.

LIMITED PARTNERSHIPS

With limited partnerships, there are two classes of partner: general and limited. Some similarities exist between general partnerships and limited partnerships:

- The tax treatment for limited partnerships is generally the same as for general partnerships.
- General partners have the authority to manage the business affairs of the limited partnership and bear personal liability for its debts.

However, the rules regarding legal liability and business management differ between the two:

- There must be at least one of each class of partner.
- Limited partners take no part in managing the active conduct of the business.
- Limited partners' liability is limited to the capital that they have contributed to the partnership.

Limited partnerships often make provision for at least some transferability of the ownership interests of the limited partners, if only through a sale back to the partnership. As with general partnerships, the ownership of limited partnerships is usually restricted to a few key employees and/or investors. To provide employees with a stake in the financial success of the business, many partnerships make use of profit sharing or phantom stock programs.

LLPs

Some forms of businesses (particularly professional businesses such as law, accounting, etc.) are prohibited from a regulatory standpoint from insulating themselves from personal liability for their professional actions. A Limited Liability Partnership (LLP) is often the vehicle of choice for such businesses.

Each state typically has its own legislation governing the creation of LLPs, and the degree to which partners are insulated from business liabilities will vary with such legislation. LLPs are taxed as partnerships, and the transferability of ownership interests will be governed by the overriding partnership agreement, but will typically be limited to sales back to the LLP, or to selected new or existing employee/partners.

LLCs

A newer form of pass-through entity is the LLC—a kind of hybrid that includes features of both a partnership and a corporation. It is like a partnership in that:

- Ownership is defined by contractual agreements among the owners, rather than by shares.
- It generally functions for tax purposes as a pass-through entity.
- The management of the organization is the responsibility of the members.

As with a corporation, however, owners bear no personal liability for the legal obligations of the business beyond the amount of money they have invested in the company. Because ownership is determined by agreements, transferability of ownership remains restricted under the terms of the membership.

An LLC can provide more flexibility in some respects than an S Corporation. For example, there is no limit on the number of owners[24], nor are there restrictions on the type of owners. Assuming the LLC elects to be taxed like a partnership, it can also offer advantageous tax treatment in connection with the allocation of income and deductions.

Under an LLC, the company can structure incentive programs that look and feel very similar to the stock plans that are often issued to employees of a corporation. The company can structure an option plan that will have most of the attributes of a non-qualified stock option. Similarly, programs can be structured that are comparable to stock bonus or stock purchase plans. Because of the tax complications associated with being a member of an LLC, ownership is typically limited to key employees who can understand the tax complexities of being treated as a partner for tax purposes. SARs and phantom stock plans are sometimes used to avoid the tax complexities associated with actual ownership

---

24 As a practical matter, however, an LLC will rarely want to have a large number of members, since this would create the likelihood that members would periodically want to withdraw from the LLC, which would impose a burdensome requirement to close its books each time and reformulate the membership agreement.

of an LLC. Leveraged ESOPs and incentive stock options cannot be implemented in an LLC.

S CORPORATIONS

While the corporate form of ownership has long been attractive because of its flexible nature and ability to insulate its owners from personal liability, a major disadvantage has always been the double layer of taxation to which its income is subject. The best of both worlds may be attainable, however, by operating as an "S" Corporation (so called because the federal laws authorizing this form of business structure are found at Subchapter S of the relevant chapter of the Internal Revenue Code). Like a partnership, an S Corporation is a pass-through entity; its income (whether or not distributed) is imputed to its owners, and taxed only once as their income. Congress designed this business structure as a form intended only for small businesses, however. It therefore set a limit on the number of shareholders that an S Corporation may have, which now stands at 75. These shareholders must be individuals, rather than corporations or other non-human entities (an exception is made for certain types of trusts, including trusts that operate as part of employee retirement plans such as ESOPs). In addition, an S Corporation may issue only one class of stock.

An S Corporation is an attractive form of organization for many small businesses. For most, the limit on the number of shareholders is unlikely to present a problem. Of greater concern to some is the fact that the corporation's income will generate current tax liability on the part of its owners. Most S Corporations pay out at least enough income to owners to cover the tax liability generated by each owner's imputed share of the company's income, thereby preventing the owners from experiencing negative cash flow. This income, however, is taxed as ordinary income, rather than capital gain.

While an S Corporation is, like an LLC, a pass-through entity, the available mechanisms for equity-based compensation are considerably broader because ownership is represented by transferable shares of stock.[25] Nevertheless, the ability to fashion an effective employee ownership plan may be constrained by the 75-shareholder limit and by the imputation of all corporate earnings, whether or not distributed, to shareholders. Equity sharing programs that might result in direct ownership of stock by employees, such as stock option or stock bonus award plans, may bump into the 75-shareholder limit if and when the company's workforce grows large enough. Likewise, direct ownership would impose liability for tax payments on employees who may find such payments confusing and

---

25 While shares of stock are theoretically more easily transferable than interests in a partnership, in reality most privately held companies restrict the ability of individual shareholders to sell their stock by the imposition of rights of first refusal, and the like.

financially burdensome (unless the corporation distributes sufficient income). While it is often possible to resolve these problems, they must be carefully addressed.

C CORPORATIONS

In terms of the volume of commerce conducted, the regular "C" Corporation is the dominant form of business enterprise in the United States. C Corporations are treated as fully independent entities, or "persons," separate and apart from those who own them. For tax purposes, a corporation has its own income, debts and tax-paying responsibilities, a feature that may result in the double taxation of income, once at the corporate level and a second time at the individual level, when the corporation's earnings are distributed to the owners through dividends. A corporation also bears sole responsibility for its legal liabilities. Of special significance is the fact that ownership of a corporation is represented by shares of its capital stock, rather than contractual agreements among the owners, and that management of the business is invested in a board of directors elected by the shareholders.

It is the relatively easy divisibility and transferability of corporate ownership interests that make the C Corporation ownership structure so popular. Subject only to the restrictions imposed by federal and state securities laws, there are few limitations on the right or ability of a corporate shareholder to sell his ownership interest—or to divide it up and sell only a part. The unique governance structure of a corporation, in which management is put in the hands of a board of directors, supports this ease of ownership transfer. While shares of stock may change hands more or less frequently, the operation of the business will usually remain unaffected, since the board of directors will continue to manage the conduct of the operations.

Because a C Corporation is free of the limitations inherent in either the LLC or the S Corporation ownership structure, its choices in the area of employee equity-sharing are greatest. Virtually any of the employee stock programs made available under the law can be adapted to serve the needs of a C Corporation. Considerations of business goals and strategy rather than the limitations imposed by legal structure will generally guide a C Corporation's selection of an equity-sharing program.

CONVERTING FROM ONE LEGAL FORM TO ANOTHER

A business is free to change its legal form. Legal and accounting considerations, as well as a desire to share ownership with employees, may make such a change worth investigating. Such a change may be simple or complex, depending on the legal forms involved. The following provides a brief summary of the issues associated with changing a business' legal form.

- **From one type of partnership to another.** A general partnership may want to change to a limited partnership or to an LLC (which is a partnership for tax purposes but a corporation for liability purposes). This is generally a simple matter. For example, converting an existing general partnership to an LLC can be accomplished by contributing the partnership interests to a newly formed LLC, which can be done on a tax-free basis. The existing partnership would then terminate, resulting in a liquidation of the partnership's assets into the LLC. This is generally afforded nonrecognition tax treatment.

- **From a partnership to a corporation.** It is also an easy matter to incorporate a partnership. The partners can simply contribute their partnership interests to a newly formed corporation in return for stock in the corporation, in which case the corporation becomes a direct owner of the assets and liabilities of the partnership. No gain or loss will generally be recognized by the partnership, any of the partners, or the corporation under any of the three incorporation techniques as long as the partners ultimately end up with at least 80% control of the corporation.

- **From a corporation to a partnership.** Some corporations may be intrigued with the possibility of changing into an LLC. Unfortunately, an existing business operating in corporate form likely will find the tax burdens imposed on a conversion to LLC or other partnership status too formidable and will opt to retain corporate status. Both the shareholders and the corporation could be required to recognize gain on the distribution of the corporation's property to shareholders in liquidation. This double tax will normally be too high a price to pay for converting. In addition, giving up the corporate form would eliminate the most effective forms of employee equity ownership.

- **From a C Corporation to an S or vice versa.** It is a relatively simple matter for a C Corporation to change its status to S, or vice versa. Such a change is implemented by sending a letter to the company's local IRS district office stating that the company has decided to change its status. The change will be effective as of the start of the company's next tax year (if notification is sent within 2 months after the start of a tax year, the change can also be made effective retroactively to the start of that tax year). Once a corporation has changed from S to C status, however, it generally cannot change back to S status for 5 years. For example, an S Corporation cannot change to C status so that an owner can take advantage of the law permitting tax-deferred sales of stock to an ESOP and then change back to S status the following year. There may also be accounting issues to be addressed in such a change of corporate status.

Appendix B
Employee Ownership Checklist

The following is meant to be a general checklist of items you will need to consider and/or do some research on before implementing an equity-sharing plan. Please note that not every item applies to every situation. If clarification or guidance is needed, feel free to contact the Beyster Institute or other employee ownership expert.

Step 1: Define a vision and objectives
A. Determine the goals to be achieved by sharing equity
B. Consider the factors that will influence the final employee ownership plan design

Step 2: Address owners' fears and concerns regarding employee ownership
A. The issue of control
B. Minority shareholder rights and information sharing
C. Dilution
D. Costs of successful implementation
E. Restrictions under any existing contracts that will affect an equity sharing plan

Step 3: Review the available tools
A. Individual-based programs
B. Broad-based programs

Step 4: Evaluate the choices and select a plan

A. Review the different plan types
B. Determine which plan(s) is best suited for the organization and its goals

Step 5: Implement the program

A. Test the approach
B. Consult with professionals

Step 6: Attend to regular maintenance

A. Keep an open line of communication with employees
B. Determine if the plan administration will be handled internally or through outsourcing
C. Review the original objectives and determine if any changes to the plan need to be made

Step 7: Ownership Culture

A. Educate employees on the financial and strategic matters of the organization
B. Involve employees in some decision-making arenas
C. Communicate with employees as to how the program is working and what the long-term goals for it are

About the Authors

David Binns serves as Associate Director of the Beyster Institute at the Rady School of Management, University of California, San Diego. A published author and frequent speaker on issues related to employee ownership and enterprise development, Binns has consulted with a variety of companies, both domestically and internationally, on the legal, financial and human resource implications of the structure and implementation of employee ownership plans. He has also been actively involved in efforts to promote the use of employee ownership as a means to facilitate privatization, defense conversion and economic development in several foreign countries. From 1984 to 1991, Binns served as Executive Director of the ESOP Association, the national trade association representing the interests of companies with employee stock ownership plans (ESOPs) and professionals providing advisory services to ESOP companies. In that capacity, Binns directed the Association's overall programs including government and public relations, publications, conferences and membership services. Prior to his work in the employee ownership field, Binns worked as a Congressional aide and as a public relations account executive. He is a graduate of the University of Virginia.

Martin Staubus is Director of Consulting for the Beyster Institute at the Rady School of Management, University of California, San Diego. He has more than twenty years of experience in employee ownership, human resources, law and organizational development. Trained as an attorney, Staubus has experience as a practicing lawyer, consultant and corporate VP of human resources. His resume includes service as an employee ownership attorney, policy analyst for Labor Secretary Robert Reich, legal advisor to the California State Labor Relations Board, and deputy director of the ESOP Association. He is currently a member of the Board of Directors of the National Center for Employee Ownership. Staubus holds a B.A. in economics from the University of California, Berkeley, an M.B.A. in organizational development from the George Washington University, Washington DC, and a law degree from Golden Gate University, San Francisco, CA.

Ron Bernstein is Associate Director and CFO of the Beyster Institute at the Rady School of Management, University of California, San Diego. Bernstein has counseled hundreds of companies in all stages of development on structuring employee ownership programs. Through his leadership of the organization's conferences, seminars and consultations, Bernstein has gained a national reputation as an authority on employee ownership and associated human relations areas of participative management, improved workplace performance and incentive systems. As part of the organization's ongoing international efforts, Bernstein has played an active role in promoting employee ownership in the privatization process in Russia, Venezuela, Egypt, and other emerging countries. He was instrumental in the establishment of the U.S. Russia Center for Entrepreneurship where he serves as its Treasurer and Secretary. He has hosted training programs for Russian business leaders to promote the transformation of former state-run enterprises to private ownership and viability in the new market economy. Prior to joining the organization, Bernstein worked for Science Applications International Corporation (SAIC) as a Senior Tax Accountant and Manager of SAIC's retirement programs. Bernstein holds a B.A. in accounting from Michigan State University and a Masters in taxation from Golden State University.

The Beyster Institute would also like to thank Alisa McMillan from Ernst & Young for her contribution to this book.

Index